Compass
&Sextant
The Journey of Peregrin Took

Phil Hoysradt
with Carol Hill

Credits
Editors: Alexis Sullivan and David G. O'Neil

Photos: Cover photo by Spencer Beebe. All photos were taken by Phil and Jane Hoysradt or Spencer and Janie Beebe except as noted. Dot Hoysradt: page 15; Norman Abbott: page 35 bottom, page 37; Dina Knohr : page 41; crew member of tuna boat: page 63; Ulrike Welsch, courtesy of *The Boston Globe:* page 157

Edited and Designed by
Story Trust Publishing, LLC
www.storytrust.com

Published by
Yankee Publishing
carolhill@yankeefleet.com

Printed in the United States of America

ISBN: 978-0-6921-8230-7

*This book is dedicated to my wife, Jane Treadwell Hoysradt,
who stuck by me through it all, and to Dot and Bill
Hoysradt, who led us, at an early age, down to the sea.*

—Phil Hoysradt

Contents

Preface

This is a story about the journey, from December 1971 to July 1975, of the 32-foot Tahiti Ketch, *Peregrin Took*. This is a brief description of her:

- Name: *Peregrin Took*, from a character in *The Hobbit*, by J. R. R. Tolkien.

- Length: 31' 8"

- Width: 10'

- Draft: 5'

- Mast height: 34'

- Engine: Volvo MD2 hand crank diesel, 16.5 horsepower

- Navigation Equipment: sextant, compass, and a lead line for soundings

- Electronics: transistor radio for receiving time ticks for navigation

- Fuel Capacity: 100 gallons

- Water Capacity: 110 gallons

- Berths: 2 single and 1 V-berth in the bow

- Stove: kerosene, wick, and pressure, with two burners

- Refrigeration: Insulated ice box

Acknowledgements

Phil would like to thank several peeople who made this book possible.

Carol Hill—without her determination and perseverance, this book would have never been done.

David O'Neil of Story Trust—for his guidance and expertise throughout this project.

Spencer and Janie Beebe—who helped make this weird idea a reality in the first place.

Hunt Searls, Ed Dyment, Kirk Hoysradt, and Carol Hill—who crewed with us along the way. Their help was invaluable.

The Route of *Peregrin Took*

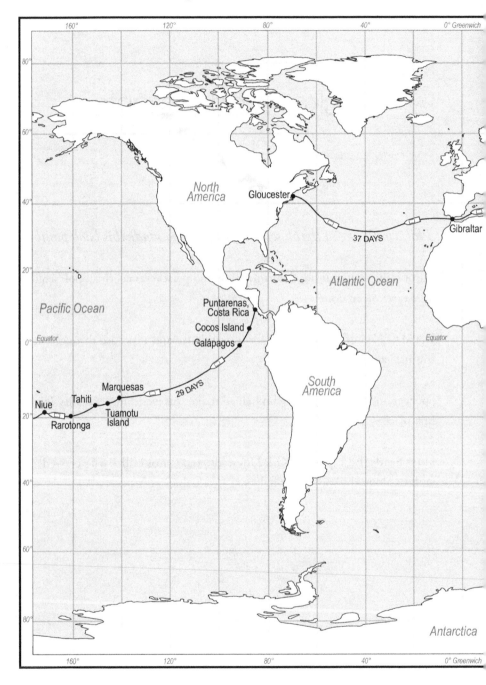

December 24, 1971 – July 19, 1975

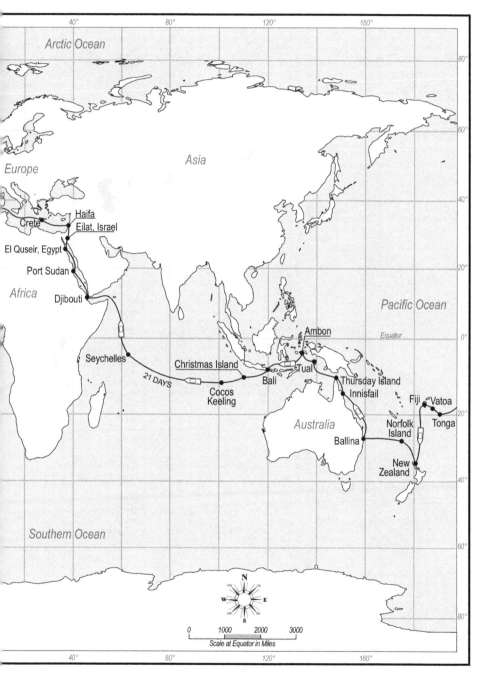

Chapter One

Growing Up Around Boats

I'VE BEEN AROUND BOATS MY entire life. I grew up near Magnolia Harbor, down a dirt road on the rocky coast north of Boston, in a house my dad built. My dad, Bill Hoysradt, was a Navy veteran of World War II. During the war, he left the "comfortable nest" of the US-based USS *Arkansas,* and boarded the USS *McKea*n, a World War I four-stack destroyer headed for the South Pacific. When a Japanese torpedo plane hit the *McKean* in November of 1943, Dad jumped off the ship's bow into the water. Many Marines died of suffocation from the burning fuel. Dad survived and continued serving, even though, in the eyes of the Navy, he had already made his contribution to the war. Eventually, the war ended, and I was born in 1947, while my dad was in Norfolk, Virginia, decommissioning ships.

My dad kept an old sailboat in Magnolia Harbor, along with a skiff. He used to take my brother Kirk and me lobstering. One day, Dad looked at us and said, "There's no reason you can't get your own traps and do this, too." In a year, I was searching the rocks along the coast after

Sailing off Magnolia, 1954.

every storm for old and beaten-up lobster traps to drag home and fix up. I
was about nine years old and ready to work, but Kirk was two years older
and wanted to be the boss of the operation. We were always fighting about
where to set the traps. Other lobstermen would turn into the harbor to
find my brother and me throwing each other overboard. The lobstermen
would break up our fights and yell at us, "The war's over. It's summertime
and you're in a beautiful harbor. What's wrong with you?"

I started lobstering on my own 14-foot Amesbury skiff when I was
fourteen. I knew I needed more money for bait and fuel, so I got a job on
a charter boat for ten dollars a day. The owner of the charter boat introduced me to Herb Ludwig, a wealthy fur salesman who needed a crewman for his 36-foot Wheeler sport fishing boat. He hired me as a mate/
captain. I say "captain" because I would take the boat by myself to meet
him at various places on Cape Cod. By the time I was sixteen I was driving a sport-fishing boat forty-five miles over the horizon, not having a clue

Phil, Carol, George, Jerri, Kirk

Phil, Carol, Georgie, Jerri, Kirk.

as to how to navigate or where to enter any of the harbors because I had never been to Cape Cod before.

By my second year working for Herb, I was starting to flap my wings and fly a little wayward. I bought myself a 26-foot lobster boat and parked it right next to Herb's sport fishing boat. I spent more time fooling with my lobster boat than doing my actual job.

Meanwhile, Herbie and I were traveling up and down the coast—stopping in Provincetown, Barnstable, and heading up to Maine. He'd say, "Tell your parents that you won't be home next week; you'll be staying on the boat." He took good care of me.

One time, Herbie was complaining and it escalated into a fight. I announced that I thought I'd best seek employment elsewhere. I remember Herbie saying, "Phillip, last year, you were worth fifty dollars a week, but this year, you're not worth fifty *cents* a week." I promptly left. Soon, my brother-in-law-to-be, Jerry Hill, hired me as a deck hand for his company, Rocky Neck Sport Fishing Dock, which later became Yankee Fleet.

Around that time, I got interested in rowing dories and started racing them in Gloucester in the international dory races between United States and Canada. It takes two people to row a dory, and Hilary Dombrowski was my partner. He was a schoolmate and fellow lobsterman. We knew each other pretty well. We lived near each other, skipped school together, went to Boston together, and rowed together. We won races at a time when the Canadians were always stomping the Americans. The adventure of traveling up to Nova Scotia on a Coast Guard Cutter and being entertained on the Canadian schooner *Bluenose* was an exciting time for two teenagers.

Oceanographer

After I graduated high school in 1965, I was lucky enough to get accepted to Southern Maine Vocational Technical Institute. I was taking a two-year associate's program in marine technology and navigation. This was a school for Mainers, and being from down south in Massachusetts, I was regarded as some kind of an outsider. I also realized that I had to study harder than almost everyone else just to get by.

An old Coast Guard instructor was the head of the school's navigation and marine technology programs. His class was very difficult and involved. Five days a week, for an hour each day, we studied navigation. Our first year, we learned seamanship and the different types of navigation. Our second year was strictly dedicated to celestial navigation and using a sextant to find our positions. Little did I realize then how useful that course would become for me.

That year, the head of our department said he got a letter from a guy at the US Coast and Geodetic Survey (now called the National Oceanic and Atmospheric Administration or NOAA) in Jacksonville, Florida, looking to employ some graduates on an oceanographic expedition around the world. Our department head had told the guy that he didn't have any graduates available yet. This was the second week in February, cold and dreary as could be up in Portland, Maine. I thought, "I've got to get this guy's phone number." That afternoon, when my classmates went to their different stations, I went out of the building and came back in through the back door. I found the note on the instructor's desk, copied down the phone number, ran the length of the campus, and called the executive officer on the ship. In a week, I was saying goodbye to my girlfriend, catching a flight to Jacksonville, and joining the crew of the *Oceanographer*, which, at that time, was the most modern, well-equipped research vessel in the world. With a crew of over 100, I was, at nineteen, the youngest crewmember aboard.

We left Jacksonville on April 1, 1967. We sailed around the world, visiting about a dozen countries. We sailed to the Azores; on to Plymouth, England; then through the Straits of Gibraltar to Monaco. When we were turned loose ashore at Monaco, we were told to behave ourselves and act as good representatives of the *Oceanographer*. That absolutely never happened! The Monacan police had their hands full dragging us back to the ship every now and then. Meanwhile, Princess Grace and Prince Rainier came aboard for handshakes and a big cake cutting. I was a side boy at the gangplank along with other crew. Some of us had our dress whites on, some of us had on our dress blues, and some of us couldn't find our shoes and were standing there, at attention, in our socks. The princess's expression was just, "Where did you get these guys?"

From there, we went to Odessa, Russia, where a few of us had our passports confiscated after we broke the local curfew drinking with the locals. Then, we went past Turkey and arrived at the Suez Canal. We were number fifty-two in line to get through and were anchored waiting our turn, when without notice, the next day, they rushed us through. We were escorted through the day before the Six-Day War began between Egypt

OSS1 Oceanographer *entering Monaco harbor, May 1967.*

and Israel when they closed down the canal. From Massawa, Ethiopia, we sailed over to Bombay, India. The poverty and congestion there were shocking. People were dying in the streets, many had missing limbs, and there was filth everywhere. It was hard going. Our crew did the first coring of the Bombay High oilfield, and I truly believe we found oil. Tapping that field eventually made Bombay into a wealthy city.

We sailed around India, across the Bay of Bengal and over to Penang, Malaysia. One night, my friend Charlie and I were rushing back to the ship on a motorcycle and we hit a Mercedes Benz head on. We were sober, too. It was a skinny coastal road, I was rushing, and the car came at me from the other side of the road. We went over the car, and I broke my leg. We were in a military hospital, run by the British and Australian air forces, for twenty-one days. The ship eventually left without us.

We were recuperating there when the first wounded Australian soldiers from the Vietnam War started coming in. Deportation was our fastest way out of the country, so we took that as our ticket over to Sydney, Australia, to meet our ship. We waited twenty days for our ship to arrive, me in a full-leg cast and Charlie, a black guy from Jacksonville, growing increasingly frustrated that the Australians couldn't figure out that he wasn't a local Aborigine. Once aboard the ship, we left Sydney for Wellington, New Zealand, then directly across the Pacific to Valparaíso, Chile, and then Lima, Peru.

By the time we reached the *Oceanographer*'s home base in Seattle, I was a pretty valuable member of the crew. I knew how to run many functions of the ship; I had been working up on the bridge for a good part of the trip. They offered to send me to any school I wanted to attend. I said, "I think I'll go back to my school in Maine and pick up where I left off." And so, in early 1968, I returned to Portland to finish my degree.

Chapter Two

Peace Corps

WHAT HAPPENED NEXT WAS PURE luck. I was struggling through a physics course—my very worst class—when a recruiter named Dave Hughes interrupted the monotony and talked to us about joining Peace Corps and working in a Central American fisheries program. He had just come back from volunteering in Panama and needed people who knew something about fisheries technology. He said, "We're working in conjunction with the Food and Agriculture Organization of the United Nations and you would be working with artisanal fishermen in one of five Central American countries."

I was sitting there with my eyes wide open. I thought, "This is the *Oceanographer* all over again. Here I am, at school, but this sounds like it's right up my alley." I went up to the recruiter and said, "Dave, I'm really interested in this, but I'm being drafted." He asked if I had been sworn in yet, and I said, "No, but that's next on my list. I've taken my physical." He said, "Well look, we can defer your military service. Your draft board won't bother you for the entire time you're in Peace Corps. But as soon as your Peace Corps service is finished, your deferment is up, and you're eligible for the military again. Realize you're being invited to train," he said. "You have to pass their criteria." Those criteria were fairly stringent. Training began in Puerto Rico in August, so they asked me to spend my summer doing something related to marine technology, to better qualify for the program. Dave warned me, "Most of the guys you'll be with will have four-year college degrees, but most of them won't have anywhere near as much nautical or fishing experience as you." He said that I would likely be sent to a port town or a city to work with the ministry of fisheries or the ministry of agriculture.

Orientation

President Kennedy established Peace Corps in 1961, so they had a few years to gather experienced volunteers to train us. All of my instructors were former Peace Corps volunteers and they knew their stuff. They were well-trained, educated, inspirational leaders. I was surrounded with the best instructors of my life. The training in Puerto Rico was an eye opener and a period of growing up for me.

I arrived at our San Juan hotel in August. It didn't take long for me to realize that my background was different than the other recruits. Their work experiences were summer jobs as parking lot attendants, mowing lawns, and such. Most hadn't been out of the US mainland. All they would talk about were their college experiences. They came from all over the country, but few came from near the coast. And they had minimal fishing experience. I didn't want to sit around the bunkroom talking about college shenanigans. That's when I met Spencer Beebe.

Spencer was a Williams College graduate from Portland, Oregon, but he was dancing to his own song. He told me he had a pet owl living in a tree outside his college dorm. He had captured and handled every bird of prey in North America, starting when he was fifteen. I saw Spencer one night and I said, "Let's go."

"Where are we going?" he asked.

"I don't know," I said.

We jumped on the nearest bus. "I've done this before," I told him. "We'll get off when we find a good place, and then we'll figure out how to get back here. I hope you can speak a few words of Spanish, because I can't. Maybe we can practice this way." So, that's how Spencer and I got to know each other—riding buses to nowhere with a bunch of schoolgirls singing songs.

Arecibo

Eventually, we were sent to Arecibo, on the north coast of Puerto Rico. We were in the rainforest where it *never* stopped raining. We were at a fairly high altitude, in an old Outward Bound training camp that had outdoor latrines and cold showers. We gathered every morning for motivational talks about what to expect when we got in country, if we made it that far. The rest was intensive language training.

We had some volunteers-in-training who had grown up in Cuba. They spoke perfect Spanish, they understood the Latin culture, and they were college educated. They were smart, capable people, and they would be sent to the most difficult sites. There was also a kid named Luis training with us. The jungle was rotten with tarantulas, and Luis started collecting them. He kept them in two shoeboxes, and once in a while, he would toss them a mouse. He was a little strange.

The camp had *casitas*, small buildings scattered around the large hall where we met for our morning talks. It rained almost every night. If you didn't mind getting soaking wet, you could walk to one of the *casitas* for a beer. So, one day, I went and had a couple of beers. I came back in the pouring rain and was one of the first guys to jump into bed. I said, "I'm not going to stay out there all night." Our beds were set up like army barracks, and mine was right behind the door.

A bunch of them stayed out drinking that night. They knew I had gone back early. It was pouring out, as usual, and I was lying there with my blanket over me. They opened the screen door with a loud whack. I heard this guy stumble and a box fall. It was Luis and I heard him say, "Oh shit, my tarantulas!" With every four-letter word known in the English language, I grabbed my blanket and ran out in the rain. I was getting totally soaked, and I could hear them all laughing from inside. Finally, one of them asked, "Are you wet enough? Come back in. There were no tarantulas in the box." Ha-ha-ha. It was true, though; Luis did keep tarantulas.

After the first couple weeks of training, our instructors decided it was time to separate the men from the boys. At this point, a lot of people were either kept in training or "deselected," told to leave. They gave the rest of us a little card with the name of a town on it and a five-dollar bill. We had no other money to speak of. They told us, "Take this money and go to the town on the card, find a family to live with for five days, and then come back."

It took me two days to arrive at the little village in the northeast corner of Puerto Rico named on my card. I could hardly speak Spanish and I relied on these little three-by-five cards with simple sentences in Spanish like, "Habla Inglés?" (Do you speak English?). Someone told me, "Bernardo does." I found Bernardo in the beautiful little fishing town they sent me to, Las Croabas, near Fajardo.

Las Croabas was a small, natural harbor with sailboats, canoes, and some bigger fishing boats. Bernardo owned one of the bigger fishing boats. He had learned English from helping the US Coast Guard lighthouse keepers on Cape San Juan, a major light near Las Croabas. He was a nice guy, and he let me sleep on his boat. "There's some food on the boat," he said. "We're going fishing in two days and we'll be gone for a few more."

Meanwhile, Tom Hunter, one of the other volunteers in training, had been sleeping on the beach about five miles away. He knew I was headed for Las Croabas, so he came and found me. He was in a bad way—bitten by bugs and down to his last two dollars. I told him he could stay with me on the boat, but the cockroaches are fierce at night. I bought a bug coil, and we shut the hatch when we went to sleep. Tom came along on the fishing trip with us. Bernardo and I sort of rescued him. Eventually, Tom and I made it back together to our training camp to relate our experiences.

Our Peace Corps trainers had a strong influence on me. Each had endured two or more years in third-world countries. They never acted like they were better than us, just that they were giving us the tools we would need to survive. They had gone through Peace Corps in its very early days, when the language and skills training were minimal. They prepared us for getting sick, which was inevitable. They told us we would get lonely and that some locals would feel threatened by us.

Choosing a Country

At the end of our training in Arecibo, we were ranked by our fluency with Spanish. The rating went from zero to four. Zero meant you didn't know what language was being spoken; four meant you could speak and understand the language perfectly, down to the accent. The scores were: zero, zero-plus, minus-one, one, one-plus, minus-two, and so on. I was surprised how many people with low scores were being sent into country. I was accepted with a zero-plus score. My previous experience with boats probably helped me get accepted. It certainly wasn't thanks to my Spanish-speaking skills.

We could be sent to one of five countries: Panama, Costa Rica, El Salvador, Guatemala, or Honduras. Costa Rica was the best of the lot. They told me I would be sent to a port town, and I learned that Puntarenas,

Costa Rica, would be a great location for me. I hounded my reps, "This is where I want to go." Most of the fisheries guys were being sent to other countries, but my reps decided they might as well send me somewhere I'd be happy, somewhere I wanted to go. I stayed with Costa Rica as my choice, and I got it. I was lucky.

When I flew down for training, I was with a kid named Tony Glavin. He had just graduated with a degree in English from Harvard. We both weighed 192 pounds. We were both sent to Costa Rica, but put in different programs. They sent him to Upala, on the Nicaraguan border, to take a census. He had to ride a donkey for four hours, then hike for six hours. There were no roads. He got some tropical disease and had to leave the country. He weighted 134 pounds when he left. They flew him up to Miami Medical Center, and he never returned.

The Fastest Way to Fluency

We went through a weeklong orientation in San José, the capital. We met the president of Costa Rica, José Trejos Fernández. Toby Orr, Peace Corps's country director for Costa Rica, was standing next to the president. He was a wheat farmer from Montana and a straightforward, good guy. He said, "Felipe," (my name in Spanish) "if I were you, I'd move into a whorehouse when I got to Puntarenas. All the girls speak English, or at least a little bit of English. Let them be your teachers. You'll learn Spanish much faster."

I went to Puntarenas and found a port town full of bars. One of the bars, Jesse's Port of Call, had a rather organized way of paying the prostitutes. The girls gave the bar half the money they made in exchange for a place to live—the Pension Royale, a little hotel nearby. They each had a room and shared a central kitchen. It wasn't exactly a whorehouse, but that's where I stayed.

I had my Peace Corps medical kit: a metal box with rudimentary supplies like bandages and sulfur powder. Whenever the police came to terrorize the girls, which they often did, the girls would grab me and tell the police, "There's a bad disease here." I'd whip out my Peace Corps medical kit and play doctor, while one of the girls would be lying there. "Get out," I'd yell, "this is quarantined!" We burned carbon in cans with little holes in the top, which we normally used as a mosquito repellant, but it would fill the room with smoke. Most of the policemen would just leave. That was one of my jobs whenever I stayed with the girls.

Peace Corps sent me to Costa Rica with two other guys in my program. We worked with the Ministry of Agriculture, in the *Sección de Pesca*, which is the fisheries department. We lived in the regional fisheries office; that was my official residence. It was a terrible place. It was meant for storage, not people. The upstairs rooms had no ventilation, only a couple windows, and it was full of bats. We could speak English among us, but the Pension Royale was way better for me. I gradually absorbed Spanish. I learned the language pretty fast once I was living in the country.

The Prison Island of San Lucas

Right across from the local fisheries office was a place called *La Playita* (Little Beach), where the poorest Puntarenas fishermen kept their boats and lived under corrugated tin roof shacks or overturned dugout canoes. Puntarenas's central *mercado* sold cheap, leftover or thrown-out food, which the fishermen would cook along with the fish they caught. Every night they had a common meal that they boiled in kerosene tins.

The three of us from Peace Corps all started getting sick from the food and water in Puntarenas. After a while, we started eating in the Chinese restaurants. They were cheap and they boiled their food. We felt good about eating there because we knew the food would be thoroughly cooked

Our dugout, Hijo de Puta, had a one-cylinder engine. We went all over the Gulf of Nicoya. Shipwrecked, stranded, and almost sunk by an eighteen-foot Manta Ray.

Our casa, far right, had a good view from the kitchen sink. Boasted water, electric, and plenty of noise from all directions until 4:00 am every day.

La Playita *(Little Beach). People also lived here.*

and wouldn't make us sick. We all lost weight. After four months, I went from 192 to 161 pounds.

Peace Corps gave my position a fancy name: fishing gear specialist. I reported to the minister of fisheries. The ministry of agriculture was working to improve the prison island of San Lucas, which was seven miles from Puntarenas, out into the Gulf of Nicoya. The prisoners had mostly rice, beans, coffee, and occasionally brown sugar or the remnants of sugarcane. The ministry wanted to enhance their diets, but it was expensive. Even though the location was better for the prisoners, all supplies had to be sent by a government launch.

The prisoners had some freedom to wander the island. They had only two requirements every day: have their heads counted in the morning and then again at night. They could carry on with individual projects, like woodcarvings, to try and make some money. Every Friday, the prostitutes from Puntarenas would go on the launch to San Lucas and visit the

Adolfo's boat and ours. We would rescue
each other from the perils of the Gulf.

prisoners. Some of the prisoners were fairly content. They would pay for the girls' services with things they made, and the girls would turn around and sell them back in Puntarenas. Usually the prisoners' families could get on the launch and visit on Sundays.

Of course, it was the warden's job to make sure the prisoners didn't escape. But they did escape—often. Prisoners would arrange through their families to have a fisherman from La Playita meet them at a beach facing Puntarenas after dark. A prisoner would walk out of his cell at night or not report for afternoon muster. Before the guards figured it out, the prisoner would be on a fishing boat headed back to Puntarenas, where his family would scoop him up and bring him elsewhere. Some would continue their disappearances, but most were found by the local authorities. Oftentimes, the prisoners who got caught escaping San Lucas were sent to the main prison at San José, which was much worse than the prison island.

Night Fishing with Prisoners

Our job was to help the prisoners catch fish. They were using a beach seine—two five-foot pieces of wood with netting rigged between. One person stood in waist-deep water while the other would paddle out in a canoe. They would run the net out in a half circle and then pull it in to see what they caught. That's how fishing was done at La Playita, too. It was labor intensive and the yield wasn't great.

So, we had the idea to make gillnets, with floats at the top and weights at the bottom with ten feet of nylon net stretched between, to catch fish at night. One of our first projects with the prisoners was making the gillnets. We started catching a lot of fish, mostly sharks, from two to six feet long. We brought the sharks to La Playita to clean them. We never used the word "shark" when we marketed them. We called it *carne blanca pura* (pure white meat) or *pescado sin huesos* (boneless fish).

We were assigned to work with some of the more trusted prisoners. I was working with two Latinos, a Costa Rican, and one tall, black guy named Chris. He was from the Atlantic side of Costa Rica, where Caribbean people lived. He was serving a life sentence. He said he temporarily went insane one night and killed three people. But he spoke English and was a fisherman, so we could communicate pretty well and he understood what I wanted to do. We had a boat, a dugout that was five feet wide by twenty feet long with a gasoline engine, mast, and sail.

We followed the currents that attracted sharks off of San Lucas. We remained in a gulf that was about thirty miles long and five miles wide, so we weren't actually in the Pacific Ocean. We went at night, not far off the island, and we would catch maybe 500 pounds of sharks. We'd pull them up in a net, unload them in the dugout, and drag it all up on the beach at San Lucas in the morning. The prisoners' diets soon changed to include more shark meat.

Our fishing adventures off San Lucas were short-lived. We ate with the prisoners, because the warden didn't like *gringos*, or people coming in from the outside and meddling with his prisoners. It took away his supreme control over them. They already had more liberties than he wanted them to have. After we started seeing success with the night fishing and getting to know the prisoners better, we thought about how we would eventually have to leave San Lucas. The prisoners would have to be trusted enough to go fishing on their own. We experimented, with some success, but then it was up to the prisoners to follow through.

One time, Norman, another Peace Corps guy, and I went back to Puntarenas for three days to catch up on other things. We came back to the prison on a Monday. The guards met us as soon as we arrived and said, "The warden wants to see you right away and he is not happy." We asked what happened and they told us that the prisoners went out fishing on the very first night they were on their own and just made a beeline for the other side of the Gulf of Nicoya and landed way down the coast. They were trying to make it to Panama, but their prison-stripe pajamas gave them away. The local police department caught them and knew they had escaped from San Lucas. So, we went up to meet the warden, and he told us our days on San Lucas were over. There would be no more *experimentos* with the prisoners. "If you ever come back to the island," he said, "be prepared for a long visit."

Before we could leave, the warden brought us up to his third-story office, where he lived above the prisoners, to show us his black and white TV. There weren't many of those in Costa Rica back then. It had rabbit ears with big chunks of tinfoil attached to the end of the antenna. We sat there and he told us, in Spanish, "I want you to see this." It was July 20, 1969 and Neil Armstrong was landing on the moon. We only understood a little of what he was raving about in Spanish, but some of it was, "This whole thing is being filmed in Hollywood. How is the world supposed to believe this is happening? Do they think the world is totally dumb?" Then he went off on us yelling, "And you people! You are all working for the CIA or something like that." Then he said, "Now you can go, but realize that man isn't really walking on the moon at all." We all said, "Okay," just to be agreeable, but we didn't know what to believe.

Like a Film Out of Sequence

Meanwhile, we were organizing the fishermen from La Playita into a co-op. We had meetings, elected officers, and were trying to get money from the food and agriculture organization to bring some fishing gear into the country. I was working with my boss, Milton Lopez, who was the *jefe de pesca* (chief of fish), to get the fishing gear in without paying duty. At the time, I thought I could just give Milton a list of what we needed, which was about three hundred dollars worth of gear, and he would send it over. But Milton wanted more money from the UN for his office up in San José, for air conditioners and typewriters. Milton told me, "Your fishing gear request is going to have to wait a while, because I need to compile my list, too." The UN's Food and Agriculture Organization (FAO) agreed to pay for some of Milton's requests, but not all of them, so Milton and company used the money allocated for fishing nets to buy air conditioners for his office. He never told me that he never ordered it, and I was left in Puntarenas getting frustrated at the customs house in San José, waiting for them to release the fishing gear that was never there.

That's how things started going in Puntarenas. We had the San Lucas incident, and then the slow realization that the fisheries office was not being very honest with us. One day, I was sitting up in the balcony of the Puntarenas movie theater watching *Zorba the Greek*. Everyone in the theater was yelling at the projectionist. First we saw reel one, then reel three, reel four, and reel two. I thought, "This is how my experiences are unfolding: reel one, reel three, reel four, then reel two." The Puntarenas movie theater felt like a metaphor for how things were going in Costa Rica, and I realized my need to better understand how the country worked.

Creating a Market

We were all getting frustrated. None of us could do the jobs we were sent there to do. But we carried on and managed to make the situation a

Gabeto after a night of fishing.

little better. La Playita was terribly dirty because everyone cleaned their fish over the sides of the dugouts, throwing the guts overboard. We were able to get the municipality to bring in a fresh water line with a spigot, which everyone liked. We didn't have electricity, but at least we had fresh water. We cooked with it and drank from it. Then we made cement tables, one for sorting and cleaning fish, and the other for storing fish on ice. There were ice plants in Puntarenas, so we could preserve the fish until the trucks came from San José to transport them. The fresh-water line and the fish-cleaning tables made the operation much cleaner.

We were making more and more gillnets, which drove the landings way up. Soon we realized they didn't need me there to catch fish or to be a "fishing gear specialist." We were landing more fish at La Playita than the

Fish-cleaning area built at La Playita for public use.

Adolfo and Phil at La Playita.

Sometimes four-wheel drive was not enough.
This rescue was made by a team of oxen.

market needed, so we borrowed a UN Jeep, put an insulated box in the back with some ice, and started transporting fish. We avoided San José, where the market was saturated. We had to go only two miles out from Puntarenas to find places where no one was eating fish. They had limited access to ice for preserving it, and most of them believed that if a fish bone punctured their mouths while they were eating, they would get an infection and die. We brought them educational pamphlets about eating fish, along with shark, finfish, snapper, grouper, and some beautiful shrimp, which were readily available in Puntarenas.

Most of the inland villages had some population of Chinese people living there from when they were brought in to build the railroads. We figured out that we could drive 200 or 300 pounds of fish for two hours or so, go into any village, get a permit to sell in the central marketplace, and then find the Chinese people. We would offer them fish and they'd buy it right away. Eventually, the people in the towns would notice, "The Chinese are buying from these guys. Something's up."

We'd look for the *carniceria,* the butcher, set our fish box up right in front of his shop, and try to convince him to buy our fish. We'd say, "We'll deliver the fish. All you have to do is put some ice on it and you can sell it within two or three days." It took a few months, but we managed to successfully sell some fish. We started making some real money. People in Puntarenas started to notice. When we first arrived, there were only two or three trucks transporting fish to San José. By the time I left Peace Corps in 1971, there were about ten or twelve, and they were all making money.

Phil with dugout.

Siempre Hay Tortuga

Meanwhile, Norman took on a project to protect the turtles that laid their eggs on outlying beaches. At night, turtles would come up on the beach, lay their eggs where the hot sand would incubate them. Shortly thereafter, young turtles would come out of the sand and instinctively go to the water. However, before they had a chance to hatch, people were digging up the eggs, cleaning them off, and selling them in the bars where people would eat them with salsa.

Norman realized that, if this went on, there would be no more turtles. The people argued, "*Siempre hay tortuga.*" ("There have always been turtles here, and there always will be.") Norman worked to educate the people that the turtles couldn't keep up with the removal of their eggs. It was one of his early projects. He traveled into remote places, from the border of Nicaragua down to Panama, and everywhere in between.

Letters from home got me through my time in Peace Corps. I went to the post office almost every day, asking if there were any letters for me. But the post office functioned like everything else in Costa Rica. Sometimes, there were no stamps for two weeks at a time. I could write all the letters I wanted, but there would be no stamps to send them. I would ask, "*¿Hay estampillas?*" ("Are there stamps?") They would tell me to come back the next day. "*¿Quien sabe?*" they'd say. ("Who knows?") I called home twice in two years. That was it. It was expensive, so I just waited on the stamps.

Chapter Three

Building *Peregrin Took*

CRUISING BOATS USED TO ANCHOR off Puntarenas with all different people—families, couples, sometimes a guy sailing on his own. I made a point of meeting every one of them. When they came to town, I would explain the lay of the land. I would warn them not to take their shoes off in town because if they walked five feet away, the shoes would be gone. I warned them to watch their boats when they anchored in certain places because people would quietly come aboard at night and take whatever they wanted. I showed them the safer places to anchor and served as a watchman for their boats. I met a lot of people that way.

I started noticing Tahiti ketches, popular home-built boats, coming into the harbor. I remembered my adventures with Spencer during Peace Corps training and started thinking about building a boat to sail away from Costa Rica with him. It was late 1969 and I still had at least one more year left in Peace Corps. I needed approval from Peace Corps director in Costa Rica, Toby Orr, to start anything. At first, I worded my request so that he thought I would be building a boat for the local fishermen. By the end of the conversation, I carefully corrected myself. I said, "It'll be registered as a Costa Rican fishing boat, but we intend to sail out of here in that boat." Toby was a good guy. He looked at me and said, "I still think it's a good idea." So, I got his blessing to start the project.

I contacted Spencer, who was living on the northern coast of Honduras. I told him, "If you can send some money, we can start building this boat." And so, Spencer agreed. I don't know why, but he did. If it weren't for Spencer, that boat wouldn't have been built. Between the two of us, we raised about six hundred dollars. That was enough, we hoped, to get the lumber and start construction. We would then dig into our allowances and figure it out from there. We both thought the double-ended Tahiti ketch would be a great idea, so I got my parents to buy the five-dollar plans from *Popular Mechanics* and send them down.

Around that time, I met Christian Knohr, an older German fellow. He was born in Costa Rica, but he was a Luftwaffe pilot and paratrooper in World War II. The English captured him fairly early in the war and put him in a de-Nazifying prisoner-of-war program. In 1947, he returned to Puntarenas. He arrived with no money at all but spent seven years building a 63-foot shrimp boat that was still actively fishing when I met him. He spoke perfect German, perfect Spanish, and he learned English while reading books in the Canadian POW camps. He was a bright guy and willing to help me decipher the boat plans. He was a major inspiration for me.

The plans, also called lofts, are blueprints with lines that show the curve in each section, or station, of the boat. Christian explained, "These plans are set up so that you don't need a large building to bring the plans up to full size." The Tahiti ketch was thirty feet long and had three-foot stations. We scaled up the plans and built the molds in Christian's daughter's bedroom. He told the fifteen-year-old girl to move into another room for a while. She was not pleased. Christian's wife, who was Portuguese, said, "Well, whatever Christian wants to do is okay." They liked me; they tolerated Christian.

The early stages of Peregrin Took. *Christian Knohr in his daughter's bedroom trying to instruct Felipe in the art of lofting.*

A Wake-up Call

After asking around, I found a man named Miguel Ordeñada, who built shrimp boats on a beach near an estuary. Miguel was good at finding lumber, and I took his advice on which type of wood worked best for each part of the boat. I drew up a contract to get Miguel's help, which ended up being naïve of me. The plan was to have various boats from around the coast bring in the wood, and then Miguel would have it milled, floated to the boat site, and dried there. The wood for the keel, which the Costa Ricans called *cortez negro*, was heavier than water, so we would need to float it in on drums.

Miguel, boatbuilder, and his shop.

I went to Honduras to give a demonstration on how to use a monofilament gillnet, and I remember seeing Spencer and showing him the fancy contract I had drawn up for Miguel. It had all these figures and everything made perfect sense. I remember thinking, this is going to be easier than I expected. When I came back to Costa Rica two weeks later, people immediately came up to me saying, "Miguel has been drunk for two weeks." I went to Miguel's family and they said, "Well, Miguel hasn't been home for two weeks, either. He's *borracho*." Drunk.

"What about the boat," I asked. "What's been done?"

"Nothing," they said.

I finally located Miguel. His wife got him home to his young children and he sobered up.

That was my wake-up call. When everyone said he was *borracho*, he was actually looking for wood, but drinking was his first interest. The locals assumed he was "off on a drunk" whenever he was gone for a long time, which wasn't far from the truth. They said he was *muy informal* when it came to boat building. I said, "I don't care if he's formal or not formal." I just wanted to build my boat. *Informal* had a different meaning in Costa Rica. They were saying that Miguel was indifferent. He did things in his own way, not my way or anyone else's. The job would eventually get done, but definitely not as I outlined in my carefully crafted contract.

Miguel had a band saw and an electric cord, so we could cut up some logs and timber, and we had a water spigot. That was all we had at the boat-building site. We had no shed for locking up tools or anything like that. We had to bring everything home at night. We brought all the materials for the boat by bicycle. If I bought two and half kilos of nails and we didn't use them all that day, I had to bring them home with me or they would disappear.

A Very Strong Cart

Nothing was easy. As we were bringing the molds from Christian's daughter's bedroom down to the boat-building site on the beach, about a half mile away, I hired a guy with a donkey and a *carreta*, a cart with wheels, to carry the molds. They were pretty big, about ten feet wide. I asked him to be as careful as possible so as not to twist or jar the molds. Everything needed to match up, stay plumb, for the molds to work. I said, "We'll do two at a time," because we had to be careful. "No, no!" he said. "My cart is very strong! We'll do them all at once." He wanted to carry ten sections at once. I shook my head, but he insisted. I don't know why I eventually agreed with him, but I ended up walking behind the cart, trying to keep everything steady. Of course, the side of the cart collapsed and all the molds tumbled into the road.

Boatbuilding on shifting sand near the ferry terminal out on the point.

We had to bring all the molds back to Christian's house, back into his daughter's bedroom, and get everything perfectly square again. I hired someone else to carry the molds to the site the second time. Building the boat was on par with everything else I did in Peace Corps—everything took two or three tries. When we completed something in two tries it felt like a feather in our caps, in the rare times it happened.

We brought the lofts up to size, made the molds, and set them up on the keelson, stem, and horn timber.

Eventually, things rolled along, and the boat was slowly built. People with boat-building experience in the United States started giving us advice, so we started deviating from the blueprints. They suggested to strip-plank the boat instead of putting on carvel planks. Strip-planking is a simpler form of construction with smaller strips of wood that are glued and nailed together, while carvel planks are tapered at both ends and bent to make double-ended boats. It would have been much easier if I had chosen to make a square transom or a boxier boat, instead of a double-ender. *Peregrin Took* was a difficult boat to build.

Framing the boat was another project. Everyone recommended laurel wood, so we got that and dried it. We ended up drying it for too long, so we had to steam it in a big box, which took about two weeks to build. We were working with all the squared-up molds secured to the keel. Ribbands held everything together. We cut notches into the keel and started bending two-inch by two-inch sections of laurel inside the ribbands to form the skeleton of the boat. The laurel didn't bend like everyone said it would, so the frame started breaking. About half the frames broke and were unusable, so we had to make new ones. We started cutting the laurel sections down the middle, especially on the more radical curves of the boat, then gluing and screwing the laurel pieces together. This seemed to work, but once again, it was trial and error.

Disregarding the Usual Way

After we had followed the molds to create the framing and put the deck beams in with an opening for the cabin, it was time to surround the boat with planking. Usually, boat builders start by putting in the garboard, the planks next to the keel, and then go up the hull. We chose to leave the garboard out so we could sweep the wood shavings out the hole every night.

About six months later, after strip-planking.

We also decided to cut all of our lumber into one-and-a-half inch wide by one-and-a-half inch thick strips, with scarfs—diagonal cuts for the joints—for the ends. Usually, people cut these planks about eight feet long. Long strips are easier to manipulate by unskilled laborers working by hand, which is all we could afford to hire. The shorter pieces, glued and nailed together, also made it a stronger boat. I was pleased with these decisions because I could hire people to help, and as long as I was master of ceremonies, everything went along okay.

We nailed the planks down instead of using screws, because we couldn't find screws in Puntarenas. We wanted to use all local materials to avoid importing anything, which would have been cost prohibitive. We made our own galvanized bolts by hand. Then we got a threading machine and put the threads on by hand. Puntarenas is one of the biggest boatbuilding sites in Central America, so I could get all the materials we needed for a reasonable cost. There were some good guys running the rudimentary machine shops there, and I became very friendly with them.

Pretty soon, we had the boat planked, the deck beams on, and they looked pretty square. Next, we started on the cabin. We used lighter wood, but it was two inches thick and fastened with our handmade bolts all the way around. We put frames over the cabin roof, blocked that in place, and put down the deck.

By the very end of 1970, the boat was ready for the water. We decided not to build the boat's interior at all. We thought, "If we get it floating, we're halfway there. We can put the interior in once we get it in the water." That was a mistake.

Spencer Arrives

The boat was becoming a monster, so my Peace Corps duties took a backseat. We still went night fishing and kept selling fish, but my mind was always on the boat. In Peace Corps, we all had many projects and many ideas. Some projects and ideas went well; others didn't, but it was okay either way. With the boat, though, we were vested; we needed results. My attitude changed toward everything. I had to actually make sure we finished the boat instead of letting anyone bamboozle me into thinking it didn't have to be done.

Talking about building the rudder.

My partner, Spencer, hadn't touched the boat yet. He finished his Peace Corps work in Honduras and the boat was ready to launch when he arrived in Puntarenas. My time in Peace Corps was now coming to a close, but we had to stay in Costa Rica just to finish the boat. We thought, "We're almost there!" In reality, we were only about halfway finished.

We got the boat floating, but we were running really low on funds. We still had to build the interior, which would involve sophisticated carpentry. Everything would have been much easier if we had put in bulkheads before we planked the boat. We were doing it the hard way, so Spencer needed to start traveling back and forth to the US for money and supplies.

We dumped Spencer's little Peace Corps severance pay, about seven hundred dollars, right into the boat. On top of all that, I had to have surgery in San José to remove a kidney stone, which was expensive. Oftentimes, we were down to just ten dollars.

On one of Spencer's excursions back to the US, he married his girlfriend, Janie Magavern, from Buffalo, New York. He was from Portland, Oregon. They bought an old Nash Rambler, filled it with supplies for the boat, and drove it down the West Coast of the US, through Mexico, Guatemala, El Salvador, a tiny piece of Honduras, Nicaragua, and on to Puntarenas. In those days, that 4,300-mile journey was a quite a feat, especially in an old Nash Rambler. They had to get all the materials through all those countries without paying duty or having it all confiscated. They sold the car to someone working at the US consulate in San José, so that gave us some more money.

Spencer and Janie in dugout canoe. About the time we finished Peace Corps, the boat was launched. Some California trimaran freaks thought it would be cool to paint Peregrin Took *orange. In my absence, they did.*

I extended my time in Peace Corps for several months. I was still getting a Peace Corps salary, but my responsibilities were vague and I seldom reported to anyone. When Toby left, I remember going to see the new director in San José. He looked at me and said, "I didn't even know we had a volunteer in Puntarenas." Clearly, I was being phased out.

Favor for Favor

At one point, a director of a UN program, Bob Carpenter, an American guy I got to know, asked me to do him a favor and go off on a UN boat looking for herring. He said, "I don't know if we'll be able to pay you." I was still getting my Peace Corps salary, so I said, "You are not supposed to pay me." "Well," he said, "I'll owe you a favor." The captain was a professional purse seine fisherman from Iceland, but he couldn't speak Spanish. The crew was all Spanish-speaking, so I was hired as the *capitan segundo,* the second captain, to communicate between captain and crew.

One time, I was getting on the UN vessel and asked if I needed my passport. "No," they said. "You are coming back to Puntarenas. Don't worry." Well, two and a half weeks later, I was discharged on a wharf up in Puerto San José, Guatemala. I had to find my way back to Costa Rica with no passport. My Peace Corps ID had my picture on it, which got me out of the airport, but they wanted to inoculate me. I argued it, so they kept me at the customs holding area. They said, "We are sending you wherever that next plane is going. You are out of here." I was deported from three countries in one day—Guatemala, El Salvador, and Nicaragua—on my way to Costa Rica. When I got to Costa Rica, they wanted to give me more inoculations and hold me there too, but I called the Peace Corps office and they vouched for me. I was able to land safely in Costa Rica.

Later, Spencer went down to Panama and he used the trip to look for an engine for the boat. He found a new two-cylinder hand-crank Volvo diesel engine with a marine transmission on it in a hardware store in Panama City. The owner agreed to sell it to us for nine hundred dollars. We just had to get it back to Costa Rica. That same engine would have cost us twenty-five hundred dollars in Costa Rica.

I wrote to my UN friend, Bob, who owed me the favor. The tuna seiner was going through the Panama Canal and returning to Puntarenas for repairs. I asked, "Can I have somebody load some stuff onto the boat as part of your machinery and then you bring it all here?" He said, "I don't see why not."

I went to Panama and paid for the engine while a Peace Corps guy from our training program arranged to get the engine on board. Meanwhile, another Peace Corps guy at the other end of the Panama Canal picked up new sails from my brother who was on a merchant marine ship that was passing through the Canal. He had bought them for me in Hong Kong. By the time I got them, they had already travelled the world. So, we got the engine and the sails up to Puntarenas without having to pay duty on them and registered the boat as a fishing vessel so we didn't have to pay a tax. That was how things were done.

As I started to separate from Peace Corps, we hired a really good carpenter to work on the boat and watch it while I delivered a yacht from Panama to southern California for a little bit of money. When I left that job, I flew back to the East Coast to Manchester. I got a job lobstering on the continental shelf and Georges Bank. I stayed with two or three people, to live as cheaply as I could. Then, I'd go back to Puntarenas, live on the boat, and continue the project. I did this round trip two or three times while the boat was being finished.

Poncho the Monkey

At one point, I was given a young spider monkey. We named him Poncho and I took him everywhere. I didn't realize what a pain owning a monkey could be. This little guy was a terror. He was fine being with up to three people, but if four or five people showed up, he'd become very agitated. I would try to walk him up the dock to the streets of Puntarenas, and he would go crazy. He could destroy a room in thirty seconds, tearing all the books off the shelves, everything off the walls. I kept him on a leash with a little line around his neck. If he got loose, I couldn't catch him in a hundred years.

I didn't have to feed him, though. We kept our boat in an estuary right next to the *mercado central*, where they threw all the old, rotten vegetables and fruit into the river. Poncho would hang by his tail off the wharf and eat twice his body weight every day. If he ever did get hungry, he would go after our food. If we confined him to the deck, he would stick his tail through the porthole, grab our food from the counter, and eat it.

If we did anything repetitive, like sawing, sweeping the floor, hauling up the anchor, he got out-of-control mad. Whatever was making the motion had to stop, or he would get madder and madder. One time, I was

Poncho was given to me by a couple of gringos leaving country. When I got a job delivering a boat from Panama to California, I passed him off to Spencer and Janie. The monkey ran their lives as he had done mine. At right, Poncho looking for lunch on the outgoing tide. He usually dined pretty well.

Poncho during a brief quiet time.

cranking the anchor up with our windlass, and Poncho was jumping all over the place. He kept trying to get at it, so I threw him overboard. He climbed up the bobstay and bit the anchor chain so hard that he broke his teeth.

After a while, Spencer and Janie arrived with some money they had saved in order to work on the boat. I said, "Well, I'm out of money, I have to go back to work. And, by the way, his name is Poncho. I'll see you later." Janie was terrified of Poncho at this point. One day, Janie was sweeping up while they were working on the boat. Poncho came down from a small nearby pier, started screaming, grabbed the broom out of her hands and threw it down. The monkey definitely had personality, so we had to be careful.

Chapter Four

Costa Rica to Tahiti

INALLY, WE GOT THE ENGINE going, the sails working, and the rigging done. Spencer's father bought us a sextant and had it shipped to Puntarenas. Getting it through customs was a battle, but it was a great gift. We were ready to go. But we realized we couldn't go overseas with Poncho, so we eventually gave him to a new Peace Corps volunteer. All told, we spent just shy of ten thousand dollars on all the labor and materials to get *Peregrin Took* underway in December 1971.

My sister Carol had arrived from the US with supplies and some money. She helped us finish working on the boat for a few weeks, and then Spencer, Janie, Carol and I took *Peregrin Took* for a test run up the coast to Nicaragua for a few days. After a successful trip, we sailed out of Puntarenas on Christmas Eve. Three and a half days later we sailed into Chatham Bay at Cocos Island, an uninhabited island 300 miles off the Costa Rican coast. We had a 16-horsepower diesel engine, a 100-gallon tank of fresh water, and a kerosene wick stove that went out if you blew on it. We had an old Plath compass from a wrecked boat, along with the

*Carol and Felipe in dugout off the Bat Islands
near the Nicaraguan border.*

Peregrin Took *on the* estero *(estuary), Puntarenas.*

sextant. Nothing on the boat was fine-tuned, but it worked. The boat did six knots, tops, with a good wind. It was comfortable and built strong. We spent about four weeks on Cocos Island fishing and working on the boat. We hadn't seen any other people or boats and we were living off the ocean catching lobsters and fish. This was the beginning of our trip around the world. We never had any intention of sailing the globe while we were building the boat or even when we started out on that Christmas Eve. It just happened. At one point it just became better to keep on going than to turn around and come back.

Cocos Island—Doña Dina *in Chatham Bay*

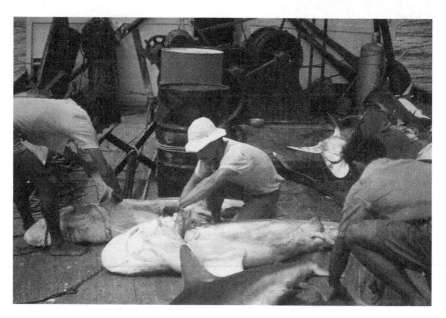

White tip Oceanic sharks caught off Cocos Island, on Christian Knohr's boat Doña Dina. *Trips to Cocos Island lasted from three to four weeks.*

Catching wahoo for shark bait off Cocos Island.

*Waterfall on Cocos Island, about halfway to Galápagos
from Costa Rica. We spent a month there.*

Carol: Never Been to Ecuador

IN THE SUMMER OF 1971, I worked in Gloucester on charter boats for the Yankee Fleet. The owner (and my future husband) was Jerry Hill; I had worked on Jerry's boats every summer since I was fourteen. It was a great summertime job.

In November, I bought a plane ticket, packed my bag with supplies Phil needed, and flew to San José, Costa Rica, where I met up with my brother. We boarded a train full of goats, chickens, ladies with baskets of fruit on their heads, Costa Ricans crowded into every car, and headed for Puntarenas. I loved traveling and I loved boats, so I knew this was going to be a great adventure. And that it was.

Soon after I arrived in Puntarenas, Phil took me to his favorite hangout: Jesse's Port of Call. We were sitting at the bar having a soda and some ceviche when a guy comes along and asks me for my health card. Health card? What health card? The guy thought I was a prostitute!

"Wait a minute," I protested, "I'm just a tourist."

He replied, "We don't do tourists here. Out!"

So that's the first—but not the last—time I got thrown out of a place being accused—wrongly, I might add—of being a call girl.

I should point out that, while I've spent a lot of time on the water, I've never been on a sailboat except my dad's, as a kid. Along the way, soon after we departed Puntarenas, it was my turn to be on night watch. It was just a beautiful night, and I was thinking, "Hey, this is pretty good." I was sitting in the cockpit with my hand on the tiller enjoying the clean ocean air, the sound of the sails, and the blanket of stars overhead, when suddenly, seemingly out of nowhere, a huge booby bird—about the size of a large seagull—landed on my head. It scared me as much as I scared it. It quickly took off, circled around, and landed on the deck. He stayed with us all the way to Cocos. We were both looking for an island to get some rest.

Lobsters on Cocos Island.

After a few weeks on Cocos, it was time for me to head back home to go back to work. An American tuna boat, the *Aires*, which was a Chicken of the Sea vessel, happened to come into the bay. They were headed to the Galápagos and mainland Ecuador, then back to a Puntarenas cannery. The captain agreed to drop me off in the Galápagos, where I could catch a flight or boat to Ecuador and then fly home. Peregrin Took wouldn't be getting to the Galápagos for another few weeks, and that was uncertain.

Phil knew the captain and some of the crew and figured
I would be safe. We didn't know it at the time, but another
American tuna boat had recently been seized by Ecuadorian authorities for fishing within the 200-mile coastal limit. To make
matters worse, the boat had gotten into a gun battle with the authorities, and an Ecuadorian guard was killed. Tensions were
running high and the authorities were on the lookout for other
American tuna boats.

I said adios to Phil, Spencer, and Janie, and boarded the *Aires*.
I got settled into my cabin only to discover that a nine-year-
old stowaway, a Mexican boy named Armando, was sleeping in
my cabin. Along with watching the seals and the wildlife of the
Galápagos, Armando served as the on-board entertainment.

After being in Ecuadorian waters a few days, an Ecuadorian
Navy ship came down on us in the middle of the night. With
huge, blinding spotlights on us we hear, "Stop where you are!
You have now been seized by the Ecuadorian government." The
Ecuadorian Navy gunmen, with helmets and machine guns,
boarded us and captured the vessel claiming we were fishing
illegally in their waters.

They stationed guards around the vessel and explained that
the vessel and crew were being seized. We would be escorted into
Salinas, Ecuador. I explained that I wasn't part of the crew and
was leaving from the Galápagos to go back to the States. They insisted I remain on the vessel and continue on to Salinas. When we
docked in Salinas, an official from the American consulate came
on board and was somewhat astounded to find me on board.

"What are you doing here?" he asked, a bit incredulous.

I said, "I was just hitching a ride."

He told me, "We've got to get you off of this boat, otherwise you'll end up in prison with the rest of the crew." I later learned that they did go to prison for six months.

Carol holding military guard's
machine gun after being captured

The American official told me the plan to get me off the boat. "Just take only what you can carry," he said. "Bring your passport, but don't carry anything extra." He told me to be at a certain spot on the side of the boat at 2:00 am. He said, "You'll hear a little knock. You're going to flip over the side, and we're going to get you off of the boat." And so, around 2:00 a.m. I went to the place on the deck and here comes this small boat with two guys paddling. Over the side I go, and they throw a tarp over me. A car was waiting for us at a dock where we landed and they took me to the American embassy. I stayed there for eight days.

I couldn't leave the embassy compound, but they treated me wonderfully. Mostly, I played with the ambassador's kids all day and just laid low till the dust settled with the authorities.

After about a week, they said to me, "All right, we're going to get you out of here." We left Salinas and drove to Guayaquil, where I was supposed to fly to Quito and then to Miami. However, the plane broke down and I had to stay overnight in Guayaquil.

The consulate had assigned me an escort for the trip back to the States. When the embassy found out the plane had broken down they made a hotel reservation for me and told the escort that we would fly out the next day. I was to meet the escort on the side-walk in front of the hotel in the morning. Well, I got to the hotel, went to the front desk, and told them who I was. No reservation, no nothing. And my escort had already taken off! I'm thinking, "I'm not going to pay for a room, it's too expensive. I'll just stay in the lobby area and hang out till morning." Besides, I have spent more than one night sleeping in an airport, so this didn't seem so bad.

I was sitting in the lobby and met two English guys from 3M company who were working in Guayaquil. I just started chatting with them and told them my story. They said, "Well, we've each got two beds in our rooms. Why don't you just take one of our rooms?" I said, "That would be wonderful." I took the key to one of the rooms and settled in for the night. At 1:00 a.m. I'm sound asleep and the phone rings. It's the hotel front desk.

"Is this the American girl?"

I said, "Yeah."

He said, "You need to leave. You prostitute."

"Wait a minute," I said. "One of the guys from 3M company—"

"No, no, they cannot do that. Out!"

And so here I am out on the sidewalk waiting for my ride to come in the morning. My ride came along and we flew up to Quito and then to Miami.

When I arrived at Miami airport I never went through immigration or customs. Instead, I was escorted through a side door out of the airport. In my passport I have never officially entered Ecuador nor exited and reentered the US.

The Galápagos

Spencer, Janie, and I decided to sail to the Galápagos, 600 miles away. We left Cocos on January 21, 1972 and arrived on January 29. We obtained a visa from the Colombian consul in Puntarenas, and we cleared with the Ecuadorian authorities. We paid the thirty-dollar entrance fee, used a hand-crank sewing machine to make a courtesy Ecuadorian flag, and they left us alone. They told us, "You can sail around the islands now. Just tell us when you're leaving." That was it. We had a great time traveling around the Galápagos islands.

During our stay, Janie's parents came to visit, and at the same time we made the decision to continue heading west. We also learned that Spencer had gotten into Yale's graduate school of forestry. Janie and Spencer decided they wanted to first sail to Tahiti and get off there to go back to the States. Since I was down to about one hundred dollars and knew that the French didn't take kindly to foreigners working in Tahiti, I planned to go back to the States with Janie's parents and work while Janie and Spencer sailed on. I would need to get a new crew once I made some money and flew to Tahiti to rejoin the boat.

*Galápagos's Kicker Rock, which we sailed through
with visiting Ecuadorian school teachers.*

*Janie Beebe with Lucero (Lightning) bringing
back supplies from Progresso, Isabela.*

I went back to Gloucester and went fishing in the middle of winter on a dragger out on Georges Bank. I lived at home with my parents in between my two trips out on the vessel. Those trips were beyond what I could endure, especially after being in the tropics for three years. I switched to day fishing, which I could handle better. It was a tough experience for me, but I managed to save some money.

I stayed in touch with Spencer through letters. I eventually got one saying they had made it to Tahiti in one piece, even though they broke the mast along the way. I flew back down to rejoin *Peregrin Took* in July 1972. About a week later, Spencer and Janie flew back to the East Coast.

Masked Booby and Marine Iguana, Galápagos.

*April 22, 1972—After a twenty-nine-day passage
from Galápagos to French Marquesas, Spencer
lands the fish but the mast breaks in a jibe.*

*A formidable task—building a new mast from seven-foot
pieces of dunnage, on Nuku Hiva, French Marquesas.*

*Janie Beebe making a flag on a
hand-crank sewing machine.*

The following pages contain an excerpt from Spencer Beebe's 2010 book *Cache: Creating Natural Economies*, which recounts his memories of the trip.

Learning as You Go

One day, about a year into Peace Corps, I got a letter from a friend named Phil Hoysradt with an ultimatum. Phil had bought plans for a Tahiti Ketch from *Popular Mechanics* for $10 and he was going to build it. If I wanted in, he'd need $500 right away. If I wasn't in, that was fine, he said, but he wasn't going to mess around.

I'd first met Phil in 1968 at Peace Corps training camp in Puerto Rico, both of us part of the 55 new trainees in the Peace Corps/United Nations Food and Agriculture Organization's Central American Fisheries Project. He was a serious fisherman from Gloucester, Massachusetts, and had sailed around the world on an oceanographic vessel. We kept in touch while I was posted in Honduras and he was stationed in Costa Rica and hatched an idea: after the Peace Corps, we'd use our readjustment allowance to buy a big dugout canoe, fix it up, and sail back up the coast to Oregon. So the ketch idea wasn't a total surprise and, given Phil's experience, seemed like a good bet. I sent him the money.

Over the next year, Phil got the hull roughed out with the help of master local carpenters. It was about one-third finished when, my stint with the Peace Corps over, I went down to join him. Janie Magavern, my girlfriend from college, came to Costa Rica shortly thereafter. She was no stranger to my harebrained schemes. Our first date had been a weekend trip to the Shawangunk Mountains, a famous rock-climbing spot near New Paltz, New York. Two friends, Teddy Ragsdale and Dave Rutherford—better known as "Rags" and "Rut"—and I were heading up there in my '63 red and cream Volkswagen bus. We had kayaks on the roof and Rut's great horned owl Archimeades inside. I called and explained the game plan to Janie and she said, sure, she'd go. Her response to the boat idea was pretty much the same. In short, Janie was game, and so now there were three of us working on the ketch.

Our shop was open-air, a small makeshift bench on the end of a dock on the estuary or "estero" side of the Puntarenas peninsula. We had one electric cord, a drill, hand planes, and saws.

Peregrin Took on our shakedown cruise off the northwest coast of Costa Rica.

We made the bolts out of brass stock that we'd tap and die. We used the lathe at the local sawmill—one that was sawing up huge, gorgeous, multicolored old-growth tropical hardwood logs rafted out of the coastal rainforest. We didn't really know what we were doing, but had a copy of *Boatbuilding* by Howard Chapelle. If we needed to mount an engine, we'd read that chapter, swing it into place, bolt it on, then realize, "Damn, that isn't right!" We'd reread the chapter, pull the engine out, and put it in again. Then, take it out and do it a third time, by which time it generally worked. At one point, Phil flew home to Gloucester for the fishing season to make more money, and then it was just the Janie and myself.

They say you can get two of three basic things out of a sailboat—speed, safety, and stability. We went for safety and stability. She was 30 feet long, 10 feet wide, and weighed 10 tons (including the old railroad tracks we scavenged for ballast). A ketch rig with two masts, a four-cylinder Volvo Penta diesel engine, 100-gallon fuel and water tanks, a tiny galley, and berths down below for four compatible companions. We decided to call her *Peregrin Took*, after Tolkien of course, but also because of the falcons. What helped me convince Phil was the meaning of the words; "to peregrinate" means to wander, so, *Peregrin Took* means, literally, "took a trip." Phil had to agree that it seemed like the perfect moniker.

Janie and I were married eight months later under a large pine tree at her family country house outside of Buffalo, New York. We had the perfect honeymoon getaway; in fact, we'd just built it. *Peregrin Took* was more or less completed a few days before Christmas, at least "finished" enough to feel confident with extra wood, paint, and supplies tied to the cabin roof; we wouldn't have to spend another Christmas in Puntarenas, and set sail for Cocos Island, then the Galapagos, and ultimately French Polynesia. It was in the Galapagos that I learned I had, miraculously, been accepted to the Yale Forest School, so Phil went back to fishing in Gloucester, to make some money, and catch up with us in Tahiti. Janie and I were on our own. We had all of three months' blue water sailing between us, and we'd spent almost two years helping to build her from bottom up with hand tools, and the toolbox was onboard. We shared a sense of confidence, a self-reliance that came slowly but surely from having done things ourselves, the hard way.

We spent a week hauled out on low tides on a beach in the Galapagos, painting the bottom and putting up stores of local food and water. Finally, on March 21, 1972, Janie and I set sail west to French Polynesia, an enamored pair of 26-year-old newlyweds on an extended do-it-yourself honeymoon.

On board for navigation was a sextant, a compass and a transistor radio. So on the last day in sight of land, it seemed like a good idea to take one more sun shot with the sextant, just to practice. I'd learned the technique a month before from Phil and had practiced it from Cocos to the Galapagos Islands. At this final moment, our precise location was known, between two of the westernmost islands of the Galapagos. But this would be the last time we'd see land for a month, so I suggested, "I'll do one more drill, just to make sure I've got it." Janie was steering under full sail with the hand tiller as a large pod of white-sided dolphins swam alongside. The tropical sun was setting on a clear Pacific horizon, light seas. I took the sightings and went below to make the calculations. Except that when I fixed our position on the chart, we weren't anywhere near the Galapagos. According

Cache: *Creating Natural Economies*

to my calculations, we were somewhere off the southern coast of
Chile, ostensibly 2,000 miles south of the islands that were, in
fact, slipping past the portholes of the cabin.

It was a bit frustrating that I didn't have the hang of the celestial navigation yet, but figured we had thousands of miles to practice. We had a compass, and—as long as we were heading west,
rather than north, east, or south—on an open ocean with no shipping lanes of consequence, we had room to learn, to adapt as we
sailed. We'd adjust our course depending on winds and currents
underway. That's when I went above deck as the sun sank in the
west and flipped on the purple light on the big brass deck-mounted
Plath compass, only to see the needle listing slightly to one side
and bubbles percolating up from a leak in the seal.

"Janie," I said with determined calmness, "hand me that kerosene, the sealant, and a screw driver, would you?" Sitting in
the wheel well with a flashlight in my mouth, I fixed the seal and
filled it back up, screwed it back together, and we were headed
west-southwest into the darkening sea.

We were anxious, but crazily confident. We had a back-up
telltale compass in the galley, we were pretty sure the sun generally set in the west, and that the Marquesas were just three
thousand miles, a few degrees south of west from the Galapagos.
We knew we'd get it figured out. We'd built her from scratch, so
should be able to fix most anything that broke. It was like learning to ride a bike; just pick up your feet and get rolling. You can't
steer standing still. Move, try it out, learn as you go. Bertrand
Russell once said, "It's not important if you are right or wrong,
but critical that you are positive." He also said, "A life without
adventure is likely to be unsatisfying, but a life in which adventure is allowed to take whatever form it will is sure to be short,"
but I was trying not to think about that one.

We were hit pretty hard about five days out in the Pacific
in what was sometimes called "the all-American sleigh ride."
There are generally fair southeasterlies in that latitude, but we
encountered a week of 30- to 40-knot winds that built up huge
breaking waves off the port bow. Sailors tend to exaggerate the

height of waves, but we'd
heel to starboard in the stiff
winds, and plow up one side
of a wave and then roller
coaster down the other side.
When we were down in the
trough, the breaking white
waves were as high as the
mast, which was 30 feet.
We took turns above and
below deck, taking catnaps.
Breaking waves drove drops
of seawater through small
joints in the planking next to

Janie at the helm in heavy weather on the
Pacific passage.

our bunk. It was three or four hours on, three or four hours off
with safety belts tied to lifelines. Janie was fearless.

We felt safer as the wind increased because it stiffened the
boat and drove her constantly forward. *Peregrin Took* was heavy
built, and although it was intimidating sitting there on the hand
tiller licking rain and salt water from your face with waves washing down the deck, it gave us real confidence that the boat was
holding together and actually firming up as conditions worsened.
It was glorious at night just feeling the wind and watching the
breaking waves and fluorescent wake, listening to the rush of
water, watching the sky, and not worrying how fast we were moving. Just along for Mother Nature's ride.

Twenty-nine days later, on April 22, things were a lot calmer,
the navigation fixes had become more consistent, and things were
going swimmingly. Anticipation of land and a successful passage
had us on our toes. "I think today we're going to see Ua Huka
about 240 degrees and 30 miles off our port bow," I told Janie.
Sure enough, that afternoon we started seeing boobies and frig-
ates—coastal seabirds we hadn't seen since the Galapagos. The
water's color changed a little, lightened, and about 2:30 or 3:00,
Ua Huka was rising on the western horizon. *Ahoy Marquesas!* We
brought out champagne we'd been saving for the occasion.

Cache: *Creating Natural Economies*

You could start to smell rich, moist soil, even 10 miles off shore. Not long after, we hooked into a big wahoo—maybe 40 pounds—on a long 300-pound monofilament line we were always trolling, and landed it onto the deck and pushed it flapping into the wheel well. Just about then the wind shifted and picked up. We tacked to the north without resetting a running backstay, one that we'd put in for safety but that wasn't part of the original sail plan. Janie couldn't get into the wheel well to steer because the wahoo was flailing wildly.

The wahoo that dismasted the *Peregrin Took* two hours before landfall on Ua Huka, Marquesas Islands.

"Hey," I shouted, "we better stop drinking champagne for a second and come up into the wind a bit more." Just then there was a sharp crack and the entire main mast sheared off four feet above the deck, sails and rigging crashing in the sea and banging against the hull. Dismasted on the final 20 miles of passage! We pulled the wreckage on deck, tied it all down, cranked up the diesel, and motored slowly to a gorgeous, small, protected bay surrounded by high, rolling, grassy hills and dropped the hook. Silence. Absolute calm at last.

Learning as we went. Indeed.

Chapter Five

Tahiti to New Zealand

Meeting Jane

I HAD FOUR HUNDRED DOLLARS WHEN I arrived in Papeete, capital of French Polynesia. That was the problem with returning to the US to work. I had to get a job as fast as possible, taking whatever came my way, only to have the travel costs absorb most of the money I made.

When I arrived, Spencer was already looking for a crew for me. He found Hunt Searls, who was sailing with his father and stepmother. Hunt was a pretty good sailor, but he was trouble on land. Hunt's father had rented a Vespa motor scooter, which he asked Hunt not to take anywhere. Before the sun went down, the Vespa was at the bottom of Papeete harbor. *That* was Hunt on land.

At sea, Hunt was really good. He never complained, helped out wherever he could, and ate anything we had, always saying the food was great. He was a perfect crewman at sea. But on land, he would say, "I'm going out for cocktails," and we all knew we were in for a not-so-pleasant ending.

Around that time, Jane Treadwell arrived. I met her through Mary Lou, a mutual friend who ran away from a Costa Rican convent. Mary Lou answered an ad in a San José newspaper from an American guy, saying, "Sail off to paradise with me. Need female crew." She boarded a 26-foot boat and away they went. I met her in the Galápagos. She was still sailing with Blackie, an ex-US Navy sailor and a wild man. Mary Lou and Blackie continued on to Papeete, where we met up with them again.

Meanwhile, Jane was living in Hawaii but had an Australian work visa. She had a free stopover in Papeete, and they told her she could spend however long she wanted there for no more money than if she had gone straight on to Australia. She got off the plane just to see the island. She had somewhere to stay at the beginning, but eventually she started sleeping on the deck of Blackie's boat. That was how Mary Lou and Jane became friends. Mary Lou told Jane, "Phil's looking for crew to sail to Australia," and, for some reason, that sparked Jane's interest.

Haul out on Moorea with new crew: Hunt Searls, Phil Hoysradt, and Jane Treadwell.

Jane came to me, asking to be part of the crew. I said, "Well, we'll think about it. You should move aboard first, and we'll see how you like it." And so, that's how we met. Jane, Hunt, and I sailed around Tahiti, the three of us living on the boat. We sailed over to Moorea, a beautiful island ten miles from Tahiti, and hauled the boat out to paint the hull.

The New Crew

From there, we set our course for the sixty-mile trip to Huahine. I had stopped using the sextant when we were in the Galápagos but had to start using it again. The French charts didn't have a compass rose on them. They didn't tell us the variation—the difference between magnetic north and true north—for the area. The charts just had a little arrow, and I didn't know if that meant there was no variation or if it was pointing true north or at magnetic north. I needed to adjust my steering compass from true to magnetic north.

Hunt on watch.

Jane working culinary delights on the kerosene stove.

The night we set sail, I thought we might be able to see Huahine just as the sun was going down. Hunt was steering the course and I went up on deck. Hunt pointed out, "That looks like Huahine over there." Our course was thirty degrees in the other direction, so I said, "We're going to stay our course. I think that's just a cloud reflecting." Clouds often look like islands when they are low to the horizon, especially in the setting sun. Hunt looked at me and said, "I might not know much about navigation, but I know an island when I see one." In the middle of the night I realized we were way off and we changed course. We turned back and soon arrived in Huahine.

Our stay in Polynesia was generally pleasant. We went snorkeling, caught fish, and cooked rice. Going out to eat was too expensive. We continued on to Bora Bora, where I bought another compass, which I tried to adjust. In Polynesia, we could almost always see the next island we were sailing toward. Then, we set our course for Rarotonga, the capital of the Cook Islands, 700 miles southwest. That was our first major venture.

Hunt directing around coral heads inside reef at Moorea, French Polynesia.

We sailed into a fresh gale: a strong wind and a big sea. I had to make the sextant work and find our position. All the hanging plants Janie had on the boat tipped upside-down. Rocks and dirt clogged the bilge pump. Jane was *so* seasick, and we were sailing very fast and way ahead of our dead reckoning position. We just kept steering and pumped the bilge.

Around the third day, I got a couple sun lines with the sextant and realized we were way ahead of where I thought we were. I got more and more sights and felt confident we would see Rarotonga in the morning. We could smell the sweet vegeta-tion of the island, and when dawn came, there it was.

Bora Bora, French Polynesia.

Taha'a—we could hear the singing at the Seventh Day Adventist Church.

We stayed for about two weeks, moored stern to with an anchor off the bow. One windy night, Hunt went ashore. Jane and I slacked off the stern line and pulled up on the bowline to keep the rudder from hitting the dock. After many cocktails, Hunt came back to the boat. It was too dark to see, and Hunt assumed he could step onto the boat straight from the dock. He stepped right into the harbor. He grabbed onto the overhanging gear and climbed up on the rudder. Soaking wet, he lectured me about taking care of the crew. That was typical Hunt: go ashore, have cocktails, get in trouble, fall in the harbor, and wake up smiling the next day.

We took cold showers in Rarotonga, and the people brought us baskets of fruit for free. The first guy I met when I went in to clear customs was a New Zealander named Don Silk. He and his partner, Bob Boyd, had arrived in Rarotonga on a Tahiti ketch thirteen years prior. Don said, "My partner and I now run an inter-island shipping company with two steel ships carrying cargo and passengers." I soon learned that everyone

Wreck of Brigantine Yankee, *home port Gloucester, Mass.,*
on the reef at Rarotonga, Cook Islands.

in the Cook Islands thought highly of Silk & Boyd Trading. Don was a nice guy. They started with the same boat plans I used for *Peregrin Took.*

Rarotonga is about fifteen degrees south of the equator, in the Intratropical Convergence Zone—a band of squally weather that runs around the globe. That meant days of rain, rough waters, and gale-force winds. I was relying on the sextant and weather forecasts, which were often wrong. We waited for a good day to leave, knowing that may be our *only* good day. We liked starting off in daylight and reasonable weather.

We headed for Vava'u, Tonga, planning to stop on the island of Niue on the way. We had some rough sailing on our way to Niue. When we arrived around one o'clock in the morning, I saw only one red blinking light on shore. I should have known better. Niue was an island with only one road going around it, one village, no airstrip, and a harbor that could only be used some of the time. We found boats anchored on the lee side of the island. There was no way to get ashore, except by a rough, cement landing place where we could row in a dinghy. The island depended on Union Steamship Company from New Zealand.

Jane trying out outrigger on Niue Island.

Cluetta and Calypso

We stayed and met some friends from Tahiti, the crew of *Cluetta*—Jim, from England, and his mate, Steve, from Canada. Cluetta Jim, as I called him, was headed for Fiji. He was an old timer compared to the rest of us, having spent many years working in London for the Bank of England. He and his original crew member, Mike, were both in their fifties. On their way from the Galápagos to the Marquesas, Mike went forward to set a spinnaker pole and went overboard. He waved to Jim that he was OK. Jim went below to start his engine so he could circle around to pick him up, but he lost sight him. Jim looked for him for three days before continuing on alone.

We also met up with *Calypso*, another Tahiti ketch like ours, with Ron and Frances Mitchell and their son, Ron, Jr. Like us, Ron built his boat. The Mitchells owned a small pineapple farm near Mooloolaba, Queensland, Australia. They had planned to sail to the Barrier Reef and back years ago, but made it up to New Guinea, then somehow ended up in Hawaii. They met some people there who convinced them to sail to Alaska. They stopped and worked for a while in Alaska before sailing down the coast of British Columbia, along the West Coast of the United States, past Mexico and Central America, through the Panama Canal, up to Tampa Bay, then around Florida to Norfolk, Virginia.

When they were in Norfolk, they got news that their daughter was getting married to an Englishman. The wedding would be in England, so they sailed across the Atlantic. After the wedding, they decided to return home to Australia across the Atlantic, down through the Panama Canal, out to the Galápagos, and across the Pacific. We first met them in Tahiti and caught up with them again in Niue. Ron told us about where they lived in Mooloolaba, saying we would be able to find work there. They had been away for seven years and travelled 56,000 miles. The Mitchells became a bit of a novelty in Australia as some of the most travelled sailors that country ever produced.

We reconnected with the Mitchells at the tail end of their trip, so Ron had a lot to say about sailing and navigation. I wanted to go through a gap in a chain of islands in the Lau group on my way to Suva, Fiji, but Ron advised me against it, and for good reason. He said the islands were all dark and impossible to distinguish from each other at night.

We learned about an outbreak of disease on Niue that had killed ten people in two months. The doctor had to wait for the New Zealand freighter for all information and supplies. He couldn't determine why they were dying. He said, "Under normal conditions, we'd be able to identify the disease and find treatment for it. But, at this point, we don't know what they're dying from." The New Zealand freighter arrived while we were still there.

We left with *Cluetta* and *Calypso* a few days later, headed for Vava'u. Whenever we sailed with other boats, it was rare to actually keep sight of them. We just agreed to sail in the same direction and hoped to see each other at the next stop.

King Taufa'ahau Tupou IV

It took four days of no sights, and the current pushing us further south than I realized, to get us to Vava'u. But we recognized the island, went around the north side, and entered a perfectly beautiful harbor. We were there for King Taufa'ahau's annual agricultural exposition.

The King of Tonga, also called King Tupou IV, was a good man. He took good care of his people. He was over six feet tall and weighed, at one

King of Tonga.

point in his life, over 440 pounds. He loved to surf and used a surfboard specially made to carry his weight.

Tonga is part of the British Commonwealth, and the king would travel to England to visit Queen Elizabeth. He would travel on an old Bank Line tramp steamer full of dried coconuts. He would stay at Buckingham Palace, then get back on his boat and bounce halfway around the world on his way back to Tonga. It was a six-month journey.

King of Tonga's private transport with over a hundred or so passengers.

Tonga is a chain of islands that runs basically north to south. It has three groups, the northern Vava'u group, the Ha'apai group, and the southern Nuku'alofa, where King Tupou lived. The agricultural visit was just a trip to the northern group. They used to have an old tugboat that towed a barge with supplies from American Samoa, but they lost the barge a year or so before we arrived. They used the tugboat to carry the hundreds of people travelling among the islands. There were no life jackets, head counts, or any safety measures.

We became friendly with Captain George, captain of the tugboat. Whenever King Tupou was not aboard, the captain became king. King Tupou always wanted to go swimming, and the captain would allow him only if they had time. Captain George enjoyed our company for some reason, so he let Jane use the king's shower, which was the only freshwater shower available at the time.

Hove To

We left Tonga, heading for Fiji. We had three days of no sights before we spotted an island around dusk. I thought it was one of three islands: one with an atoll that would be on our left, one on our right, and one with clear passage through. I thought it was the one with clear passage, but I wasn't positive enough to risk sailing up on the windward side of an atoll at nighttime.

We hove to—a technique of adjusting the sails and the helm so that the boat maintains its position—and spent the night crashing up and down in the wind. When light broke the next morning we saw an entirely different island than we expected. It was more low-lying, so I got out my old sailing directions and figured that the current carried us further south than I realized. I wanted to be sure it was the island I thought it was so we could get a better handle on our navigation.

We went around the back of the island, through a thirty-foot wide pass in the reef with no breakers. It looked shallow, but we got in with our five-foot draft and anchored inside a reef behind the island. By the time we were inside the reef, I knew we were in the southernmost island of the Fiji group. I got a couple sun lines and knew where we were.

Sun Lines

We figured out our location through sun lines by using our short-wave radio to get the time-tick broadcast from Boulder, Colorado; Hawaii; or the BBC's report from Big Ben in London. We would then measure the distance between the very bottom of the sun and the horizon. If we could get a sun line in the morning, which we did that day, we would combine that with our assumed, or dead-reckoning position. Then, we followed the sextant as the sun crept up to its highest point. When the sun reached directly overhead—and it always seemed to hang there for five or six seconds before it slid down again—we were able to determine our latitude, called a noon sight.

We then used our running fix, advancing our line of position with our estimated speed, to get two crossing lines. If we were five miles within where I thought we were, I considered that pretty good, but sometimes we were twenty miles away from where I thought we were. With unpredictable ocean currents and difficulty getting celestial fixes, we risked more inaccuracy than normal. It was especially difficult near Fiji, where we had constant ocean currents that often ran faster than a knot. So, I wanted to go ashore and have the locals verify our position. Hunt liked to joke about always needing to stop and ask the locals where we were.

We arrived on the southern-most island of the Lau group. Locals came to meet us on their outrigger canoes. It was a fairly primitive island, with no airstrip, and reefs that kept bigger boats from stopping in. Trading schooners, which came maybe once every few months, had to send flat-bottom skiffs through the reef. That supplied the island with any goods they couldn't grow themselves.

We spent the afternoon spearfishing inside the reef. The locals were friendly and caught enough fish to feed the whole village for one night, including a good-sized leopard ray that we didn't want to eat. They left us with too much fish. We didn't have refrigeration, so we dried some and ate what we could. We stayed a few days then ventured on.

Salty Brew

We passed some volcanic islands as we finished our route to Suva. We had good position reports, even though our sights were few. We found Suva. When we checked in we avoided mentioning that we'd stopped in the Lau group, which was not allowed, and we got permission to land. We had to let them know when we were planning to leave, but they let us stay in Fiji for as long as we wanted. We anchored in Suva harbor and rowed to Suva Yacht Club, where we learned of an out-of-season hurricane coming our way.

Once we got better information about the hurricane, we moved to a more protected anchorage in front of the Trade Winds Hotel. We wanted the first pick of spots in the protected anchorage. I put down three anchors, getting ready for a huge blow. Meanwhile, most people were denying the hurricane would ever come, because Fiji hardly ever got hit, especially a month out of season. For some reason, we heeded the warning. A day before the hurricane, reports came that it was headed right for Viti Levu, the island where Suva is located. All the local trading boats started piling up in front of the Trade Winds and taking refuge up mangrove-filled creeks.

Some American guys on one of the boats, *Salty,* from California, had been making home brew down below in a galvanized bucket. A day before the storm, they invited everyone at the anchorage over for a pre-hurricane party. That beer produced the world's worst hangover! No matter where the boats were from, everyone in that anchorage was badly hungover from the *Salty*'s brew, including my crew and me.

Hurricane Bebe

Hurricane Bebe hit Fiji on October 23, 1972. Most sailors stayed aboard their boats, even the Fijian copra boats with poor anchoring equipment. Mangroves lined the coast and it wasn't rocky, so it wasn't too dangerous. I may have been over-anxious or maybe I wanted to get up-wind, but I decided to move from the choice spot we got early on in the storm. I was pretty sure we were dragging, so we got all our anchors up before dark. I wanted to get in front of all the boats to avoid anyone dragging down on us. If we were going to drag, we would drag down on them.

They estimated the winds hit 155 knots, but we were all pretty well protected. All communication in Suva was out and all the coastal roads flooded. We learned from a shortwave station based in New Zealand that the eye of the storm passed right over us.

We dragged and reset our anchors, then went aboard a Fijian copra boat that was next to us during the eye of the storm. Around three o'clock in the morning, we were both aground in the mud. Fijians are great big people and I yelled for one of them on an outboard boat to help us. Our boat was on its side, so he helped us gather our anchors together and kedge the boat off into the bay. We re-anchored just as the eye passed. The

Hurricane Bebe hitting Suva, Fiji. The eye passed over us that night.

sky was so clear that we could see the moon. Then, suddenly, the wind shifted and the hurricane started all over again.

The three of us stayed on the boat through the hurricane, taking turns keeping watch. Flares went off all night long. No one could do much to help anyone. It sounded like a freight train was roaring past us in the darkness. The boat rocked to its side and skidded back and forth while we pulled on our anchors. We were lucky not to hit another boat or have another boat hit us. Two boats dragged past us, and we were lucky our anchors didn't tangle. Our bowsprit and overhanging rudder were both vulnerable in a storm.

Some boats went up on the reef, and the Queen of Tonga lost her yacht on the main reef in Suva harbor. We all made it through the storm okay and congratulated each other on surviving one of the worst hurricanes to hit the area. There was talk of an after-the-hurricane party, but all the boats started leaving. The hurricane was bad enough, and we couldn't even think of enduring another *Salty* brew hangover.

The Snake Pit

As we prepared to leave, Hunt managed to get in a little bit of trouble. Before the hurricane, he had gone ashore for cocktails at a bar called The Snake Pit. He said he inadvertently stumbled and spilled his beer on one of the tables where big Fijians were entertaining their lady friends. He ended up being thrown out of the bar—literally. They threw him out a window. He said he didn't remember much, but he landed softly in the hedges.

When he returned to the boat and the hurricane started, he realized he had lost his passport. After the storm, while we were preparing to leave, we were warned that Hunt needed his passport if he was going to try to get a work permit in New Zealand. Otherwise, there would be hell to pay. So Hunt went to the US Embassy in Suva with a concocted story about swimming for his life through Hurricane Bebe. When he finally reached shore, he said, he realized his passport was missing. The woman opened a desk drawer, pulled out a passport and asked, "Does it look like this?" Stunned, Hunt said, "That's my passport! Thanks!" The woman replied, "It was found outside The Snake Pit four days ago and someone turned it in."

Kandavu on a Whooze

We departed Suva without much fanfare. It was still windy after the hurricane, so we sailed all day down to Fiji's Kandavu Island, en route to New Zealand. We had a 1,200-mile sail to New Zealand in front of us, so we took refuge from the wind in the lee of Kandavu for a couple days, trying to get a weather report.

We anchored in a village that had been destroyed in the storm. The locals were rebuilding it right away. Their buildings were handmade out of thatch and bamboo, and everyone knew how to build a house. They struggled fixing the church's corrugated tin roof, which had blown all over the place. The tops of almost all the coconut trees had been blown off, creating a huge mess and threatening their principle source of income: copra, dried coconut used to make oil.

They all drank kava, their answer to alcohol. Made from a root ground into a powder and mixed with water, kava turned our lips numb and put us to sleep. Drinking it is a ritual in their culture. We couldn't walk through any village without stopping with the elders, sitting in a circle, and drinking kava. Very few words made it across the language barrier, so we just had to sit and drink kava with them. Anywhere we traveled among these islands landed us in a whooze by the end of the day. They never wanted us to leave the kava circle. They would happily sit there until the sun went down and have the women make their dinner.

We had a hard time getting through the kava circles to find a reliable weather report. They all said, "It'll probably be the same weather we had yesterday. It will be like this tomorrow, so have more kava." We went through three villages looking for the weather shack, only to find that the weather forecaster wasn't even on the island because of the hurricane. We got some flimsy weather report and prepared to go down to thirty-five degrees south latitude, onward to New Zealand.

Through the Fog

We spent eight and a half days sailing to New Zealand. We heard reports of fierce weather in the Tasman Sea, and New Zealand is famous for its gales. Oftentimes, low-pressure systems on either side of the islands would pass over us and we would get strong, shifting winds.

We were sailing in fog, which suddenly lifted to reveal these beautiful green hills right in front of us. We saw the lighthouse on Cape Brett the night before and motored up to the town of Russell, following sailing directions that told us Russell wasn't a port of entry. We tied to the pier and the constable came to meet us. We told him our boat's name and that we had just come from Fiji. He immediately got upset and told us *Peregrin Took* had been reported missing at sea. He had to leave us to report that we were safe. New Zealand didn't have a coast guard, but they put unreported boats on a watch list through the central government for all shipping merchants. They had an effective "sched" system, where boats were supposed to call in every day and report their positions. If they ever failed to do so, we would be posted as "not reported."

Hunt's father was the one who reported us missing. He was a former Naval Academy graduate and was still in Tahiti writing his book *Overboard*, which they eventually made into a movie. He was checking our whereabouts and contacted the port captain in Suva to see if we had made it there before Hurricane Bebe. The port captain said we weren't

En route to Whangaroa, New Zealand.

there. Meanwhile, I had on my boat the clearance from the port captain proving we *were* there and *had* reported ourselves. Hunt's father called New Zealand next, who put us on a watch list of missing or unreported boats.

After the constable shared word of our arrival on the airwaves, he sent us to Opua, the official port of entry. They offered us work permits saying, "If you can find a job, you can work." Hunt went to the South Island and picked tobacco, while Jane and I stayed in Russell. It was a beautiful little town and the perfect place to anchor.

The Pirate

For some reason or other, I wanted to get a job on a fishing boat. I heard about a guy in Whangaroa, who they said was pretty much a pirate and always in need of a crew. We hitchhiked the twenty miles northward, through old winding roads, one-way bridges, and beautiful countryside to Whangaroa. We landed in a town of about 175 people, located on a perfect fjord. The only hotel had twelve rooms. Some crayfishing boats operated out of there.

We stopped at the post office general store, asking for Brian Wareham. They pointed to his boat, saying he was about a mile away, down on a wharf. "By the way," the man said, "please take his mail because he re-fuses to pick it up." They gave me about five pounds—maybe six months' worth—of mail.

When we found Brian, he called out to us, "Come aboard. I'm down on the bilge." We went aboard and introduced ourselves. "I've got a pile of mail for you," I said, thinking he'd be happy to see it. "Yeah? Give me the mail," he said. He grabbed it and used it to wipe the black oil from his hands. "I don't want it," he said. "None of this mail has any good news for me." That was my introduction to Brian. He had a tendency to get in trouble. I secured a job on his boat and then we hitchhiked back to Russell.

We heard about a cat that was born on a sailing boat to a Dutch couple immigrating to New Zealand. When they moved ashore, they gave the cat to an old-timer living on a boat in nearby Matavai Bay. He wasn't doing well and had been taken to the hospital. Meanwhile, the quarantine officials came out saying they were going to destroy the cat. The cat had never been ashore; it had been in quarantine its whole life. We took her and named her Ami, French for friend, but the quarantine officials misspelled it Omi, so we called her that instead. A month later, Omi passed quarantine.

Omi and Felipe boating.

Working for Brian

After a few days in Russell, during which we acquired Omi, Jane and I sailed around to Whangaroa. Jane got a job working two shifts per day in the Marlin Hotel, making thirty dollars a week. Brian promised me one hundred dollars a trip. I agreed, thinking each trip would last a few days. I soon found out that these hundred-dollar trips could last up to three weeks.

I went crayfishing and lobstering with Brian on the *Margaret M.* for about four or five months. We fished all the way from the Three Kings Islands, thirty miles north of North Cape, to thirty miles east of East Cape, covering a distance of over 400 miles. Brian's idea of lobstering was "if that guy isn't going to fish his traps, I'll fish his traps for him." On my first trip to the Three Kings, I noticed bullet holes in the side of the *Margaret M.* We fished way off shore and I asked, "How come we don't

Marlin Hotel staff in Whangaroa, New Zealand; Jane is front and center.

just go down the coast?" "Well," he said, "I give this place a wide berth. See these bullet holes? They came from out of that bay." We fished the Three Kings alone—Brian, his girlfriend Marina, and I.

Whangaroa was a small town on a fjord, with houses on steep, terraced hills. It was full of gossip—everyone was talking about everyone else's every move. Of course, Brian always made the list of popular topics to talk about, and by association, I made it into a lot of those stories, too. I was banned from the Marlin Hotel, where Jane worked, because I worked for Brian. I snuck in for a beer from time to time. When Jane was invited for Christmas dinner, I wasn't, because I worked for the pirate.

Our jobs never paid much when we were traveling. We didn't have time to spend looking for work, so we took what was offered. We knew we would be gone in a few months—and we usually were. We went down to Whangārei, hauled the boat out, got it shipshape, and went on our way. We arrived in New Zealand in October 1972 and left on April 5, 1973.

Tidal haul-out—Whangaroa, New Zealand.

Jane and Omi catching dinner—Bay of Islands, New Zealand.

Carol: New Zealand "Fire"

IN 1972, MY PARENTS AND I decided to visit Phil and Janie in New Zealand. My parents worked all their lives and hardly ever took a vacation when we were all growing up. With six kids, there wasn't much money left over, but somehow they managed to buy tickets to go from Los Angeles to New Zealand. Dad had a homemade camper on the back of his truck, and their plan was to drive across the country. I met up with them in Texas and together we drove to LA.

Our flight to New Zealand included a two-night stay in Tahiti. Phil suggested that we stay at the Stuart Hotel, in Papeete, because it was the most affordable and was right on the quay where all of the boats tie up. It was a very old, wooden, multi-story building with a fire-escape stairway that wrapped around to all the floors.

When we checked in at the front desk, which also served as the hotel's bar, I noticed that the guy checking us in was wearing a Hawaiian shirt and faded red pants. He booked us into two rooms on separate floors. I can remember thinking to myself, "How come he has me two floors above my parents?" It didn't appear to be too busy. My room had an iron bed with just a bottom sheet and a top sheet, no bed cover. In the middle of the ceiling was a single, bare light bulb, no shade. And the door had one of those old-fashioned skeleton key holes but the key didn't work. The door had a hook-and-eye latch for a lock. The window faced the fire escape.

In the middle of the night, I heard knocking on my door and someone saying, "Fire, fire! Got to get out! Fire!" And I'm thinking, "I don't smell any smoke." I got down on my knees and looked through the keyhole and I saw the faded red pants. I realized that he's saying "fire" a little too quietly. It wasn't like he was really excited and telling the whole hotel to get out. I decided not to open the door. He keeps banging on my door, and I can see the hook-and-eye latch coming loose. I thought, "I better get out of here." I unscrewed the light bulb and broke it to use as a little weapon, just in case. I grabbed my backpack, climbed out the window, and ran down the fire escape. Just as I got out the window, the door latch gave way and he was in my room. As I'm going down the fire escape, I'm yelling for my Dad to wake up. Dad hears me and he runs up the main staircase. As he is coming up the stairs, he, without knowing it, passes the guy who just broke into my room. Soon everything calmed down; the guy was gone. I went upstairs, pulled my mattress off my bed, brought it down to my parents' room and spent the night there.

After another day in Tahiti, we flew to Auckland and met up with Phil and Jane in Whangaroa. We went sailing with them and then did some touring around the two islands for the next few weeks.

Chapter Six

New Zealand to Indonesia

Mutineers

PEREGRIN TOOK LEFT NEW ZEALAND carrying four people and a cat. Hunt came back to sail with us, bringing an American guy named Jim. We headed north for Mooloolaba, planning to take Ron Mitchell's advice to look for work there. We stopped at Norfolk Island, which, much like Niue, lacked an anchorage. Jane and I went ashore in a dugout canoe that we used as a dinghy.

When we landed, we were met by two descendants of the HMS *Bounty* mutineers. Just before 1900, the descendants had been transferred from Pitcairn Island to Norfolk Island. Norfolk was closer to Australia, so the British thought they could tend to the descendants' particular needs a little better. Even though the two islands were essentially the same—same size, steep cliffs, no landing place, rich vegetation—the mutineers became homesick. Many of them returned to Pitcairn, but a few stayed.

We asked to go to the port captain's office, but they said they had only a magistrate from England, whom they didn't like. We were the first overseas boat to come into Norfolk that year. We didn't know that Norfolk Island had a history of yachts being wrecked there. We soon realized we had to stand watch while we were there because it was such an unsafe anchorage. Phil McCoy and Frankie Christian took us to a pub, where we called the magistrate and reported ourselves.

Not So Rico

Jane and I went back to the boat so that Hunt and Jim could check out the pub and return before dark. Hunt was unsteady in the dugout. It was easy to tip over, and we didn't want that to happen to them at night. We had seen people fishing from the shore, hauling in a pretty big bronze whaler shark, so we knew the place was full of fish and sharks. We told Hunt and Jim to find the pub at the top of the hill but get back before dark.

Hunt and Jim went up to the pub and decided to stay after dark. There were complimentary bottles of wine on the tables in the restaurant section, so Hunt and Jim started smuggling the bottles whenever they went to the men's room and hiding them. They got caught, so they decided to make a run for it. The constable got wind of the situation and the two spent the night hiding out in a cold cow pasture.

Meanwhile, Jane and I spent the night in rainy, squally weather, yelling back and forth to shore. We saw a police car on shore and someone shined spotlights on us. I assumed Hunt and Jim had tipped over in the dugout and were somewhere between the boat and the landing place. Whether that happened or not, I did not know, but Jane and I stayed up all night. It was so rough at anchor that we were worried we would have to get underway, with our dinghy and two crew ashore.

As the sun was rising, Jane and I finally had a chance to lie down and rest. Pretty soon, there came Hunt, Jim, and a terrified-looking policeman in the dugout canoe. Hunt and Jim were freezing cold and looked terrible. They claimed someone stole their oars, which ended up being the policemen chasing them. They got their passports and money and rowed back ashore. They went to the magistrate, who gave them the choice between a fine of one hundred dollars Australian each, or three months of hard labor in Australia and deportation. They paid the one hundred dollars.

Meanwhile, the story was passed around the island that the greatly disliked English magistrate had met and fined two sailors on the first overseas boat to visit their island that year. The islanders were outraged. They had a little weekly newspaper that published an article with the headline "Costa Rican Vessel Finds Norfolk Island Not So Rico." The local constable took us on patrol and we dined with them almost every night. The islanders couldn't do enough for us. They gave us so many fruits and vegetables that it would take months to eat it all. Leaving was bittersweet. It was a fun place, and the islanders treated us really well. But it was an open anchorage and we needed to get on our way.

Forty Signatures

It took us eight days to sail to the west coast of Australia. One midnight, I got a rough bearing on Cape Byron light, up on a high cliff near the border of New South Wales and Queensland. The weather continued to deteriorate and we spent the entire next day very close to the Australian shore, invisible through the thundershowers and rising winds.

We saw a shrimp boat and I asked them if we were near Evan's Head, which is where I thought we were. We were right. So, I asked in the New Zealand way, "Do you reckon it's going to storm?" "I reckon it's stormin' now," he said. They offered to let us follow them into Evan's Head, but I knew that wasn't a port of entry. I told them we were headed for Ballina,

Landfall Cape Byron, New South Wales, Australia.

and they said, "Well, please yourself." We eventually found Ballina, and the huge sea, breaking over the jetties, tossed us into the port.

We entered Australia only after signing my name on forty different documents. They scrutinized everything: our rubbish can wasn't right, they didn't like that we had a cat, and on and on. They said, "You're all quarantined again." They told us that Ballina was no longer a port of entry and that we had to take our boat to Brisbane. Brisbane was hard to sail to, so Jane and I hitchhiked to the customs office there only to find it was closed, so we hitchhiked back.

Hunt and Jim got off the boat in Ballina and found jobs inland, while Jane and I got back on our boat and sailed for Mooloolaba. At the pilot station in Mooloolaba, we handed over a great big pack of documents with all our names, passport numbers, travel history—everything. The pilot said he would deliver it all to the customs office after he cleared the next ship.

On Ron's Advice

We were the first overseas boat to anchor in the new Mooloolaba Yacht Club. It cost us two dollars a week. We lived on the boat, started meeting people, and settled in. Jane and I got jobs right away, both making more money than we had in New Zealand. I worked in construction for the equivalent of about one hundred twenty-five US dollars a week. Jane got a job in a shop down the road. We both could walk to work, but I liked to go by dugout canoe.

I worked as a laborer in a housing development and then was trained as a surveyor on the site of a fifty-home development. I needed a motorbike for the second job. I was the only guy on the job all day. I had to watch all the subcontractors and make sure they were doing things correctly. Some of the subcontractors would show up with a simple tool, like a hoe, to install underground pipes. When they needed a second man to finish the job, I ended up working as a laborer again, helping the subcontractors.

Meanwhile, Carol was finishing her work in Gloucester and preparing to fly to Sydney. She was flying halfway around the world to meet us, so we flew to Sydney to meet her. We also had to go to the Indonesian Consulate in Sydney to pay the high price for visas to visit Indonesia. We got our visas, met Carol, and then headed back to Mooloolaba. We sailed up the Barrier Reef, stopping at several islands and ports on the way up through the Whitsundays.

We eventually came into a small inlet, near a town called Innisfail. It's the rainiest place in Australia, and we arrived for the wet season. If we had carried on, we could have gone up to Cairns and probably found better jobs. For some reason, we decided to stay.

Innisfail, Northern Queensland, where we worked during the wet season.

John's Story

We all found work in Innisfail. I joined a shrimp boat with a guy named John Kreystin. He took me on as a deck hand. He was a Hungarian who escaped from there under a barbed wire fence as a kid during the revolution of 1956. Years later he boarded an immigrant ship to Australia and arrived with a bunch of "blue jackets," what Australians called immigrants because they were given a blue jacket, blue wool blanket, and a few other basic needs at arrival. They would land, show their credentials, and then have the whole new world of Australia opened up to them. They were on their own from there.

One of John's friends on the ship said, "If either of us finds ourselves making a lot of money, we'll try to keep in touch with each other by mail, and we'll report every now and then and maybe we can find a real good job." John wound up cutting sugarcane in Innisfail. They burned the cane to get rid of the venomous snakes and to make it easier to cut. They cut the cane by hand; it was a rotten job. He was charred black every day. One day, he cut his way down a swath of cane and suddenly saw the deep blue of the Pacific Ocean and the pristine waters of the Barrier Reef. He said to himself, "If I ever get out of this sugarcane mess, I'm going to get a boat and be a fisherman."

Eventually, John's buddy sent a letter from the frontier boomtown of Darwin, Australia. He had a job making sandwiches but eventually got ahold of a vending machine. He filled the machine with sandwiches and put it in a central place in the town. He wrote, "I can't make the sandwiches fast enough. I'm charging three dollars each, which is way too much, but I'm making a ton of money." John wrote back, "Well, why don't we buy a boat together?" His friend agreed, sold his business for a lot of money, and came down from Darwin. John found a boat, and they both went fishing, but his friend got so seasick that he decided to go back to Darwin to make sandwiches. He told John, "You run the boat. If you make some money with it, send me some. And he gave the boat to John. John named the boat *Poltava*, after the now-Ukrainian city he lived in before he left for Australia.

John proposed to his wife by mail. Years earlier he met an Austrian girl at a dance in Hungary. He found out that Australians often got married by mail order, because there were more men than women. So John decided to propose to the Austrian girl. He wrote, "I only met you one night, but I think you're agreeable. I have some land I bought with a view of the ocean. I have a boat, and I'm making some money, but I'm by myself."

She agreed. She would marry him as soon as *they* arrived in Australia. Unbeknownst to John, she had an eight-year-old child. She wrote, "I'll be arriving in Darwin" on such-and-such a day—no mention of her daughter. John borrowed a station wagon and drove the coastal road southward nearly 1,000 miles to Brisbane, then took the highway northward 2,100 miles across the country to Darwin. He waited for ten days in Darwin but she wasn't there. He drove all the way back to Brisbane, then back on the coastal road to Innisfail, where he learned of a telegram waiting for him at the post office. He read the telegram: "Your wife is waiting for you in Darwin." He had already put thousands of miles on his friend's station wagon, but he got back in and did the trip again. He found his wife, and to his surprise, her daughter, waiting for him in Darwin. They could barely communicate but found a common language in German.

They had a son together. John and their kids spoke good English, but when I met them, his wife couldn't speak English at all. She was very shy but a good mother. And John was a good guy. We had Christmas dinner with them. His wife cooked a delicious dinner for us.

A Conversation Between Australians

One night, the river flooded in Innisfail. Carol, Jane, and I were on our own boat, and our Australian friend Alistair was sailing on his. It was hot and rainy. Alistair had come over for dinner. We were all down below and had just finished eating when I stuck my head out to see if the rain had stopped and we could open the hatch. I was coming from the cabin light below up to the pitch-black darkness of the deck. As I came up the ladder to the deck, I grabbed a bungee cord for the tiller, thinking to myself, "I usually put that away under the deck. I wonder how it got here?" Then I noticed its head turning around in my hand. I stepped backward, yelling, "That's a snake!" Almost every snake in Australia is poisonous. He must have come down the river in a pile of debris, found our rudder or the anchor chain and slithered up onto the deck and was watching us in the cockpit. Carol hates snakes, so she was petrified. The forward hatch, above her bunk, was open, so I said, "Go close the forward hatch." She was frozen. We were all in a panic. Alistair was yelling, "Kill it! Kill it!" I said, "Alistair, you go up and kill it. You're a native Australian. That's an Australian snake. Why don't you go talk to him?" Eventually, we got our primitive weapons together—spatulas and flashlights—and found the snake on the stern. We got a deck brush and whooshed him back into the river. And that's how we celebrated our New Year's Eve in Innisfail. Even though it was hot, Carol slept with the forward hatch closed till we left Australia.

Where the Roads Stop

Jane and Carol got jobs at Innisfail Hospital. Carol said, "The pay is terrible, the job is terrible, and if we are going to be staying in Innisfail for a while, I'd like to see more of Australia." She took off with a backpack hitchhiking, riding busses, and staying in youth hostels all down the Australian coast. She went down to Melbourne at the southern tip of Australia, then flew over to Tasmania with other youth hostelers who were doing the same route.

Meanwhile, Jane and I remained working in Innisfail for a few months and then sailed the boat up the coast to Cairns where we prepared the boat to keep traveling north. We sent a message to Carol, through the post office general delivery, to meet us in Cairns. She showed up, got on board, and we started sailing the rest of the way up to the northern end of Australia. We stopped at Restoration Island for a while, where Captain Bligh first landed after the *Bounty* mutineers threw him overboard. We also made a stop on Fantome Island. When we went ashore, it looked like it had been well-inhabited but abandoned suddenly. We walked around a while, wondering all the while what could have happened here to make everyone leave. There was bedding, dishes, cutlery—everything you needed to live—just left where it was. One thing we did find was what appeared to be a brand new black bucket. Just the right size to replace the worn out one we had on the boat. So we took it. Days later, while talking with some other sailing folks, we discovered the island had been a leper colony that had been abandoned for a new facility. Our new black bucket went overboard!

Sailing up the Great Barrier Reef was beautiful and mostly uneventful sailing. The islands were close enough together that we didn't have to make long runs, and the winds and seas were usually pretty calm.

Once we left Cairns, the paved roads stopped in Australia. That's where the fugitives—people being pursued by their ex-wives, the police, or whomever—went north of Cairns. Unless they got in more trouble, no one would bother them. As long as their needs weren't too great, they could remain reasonably free. Changing names and towns is common in Australia. We met many people along the way who would introduce themselves as John in one place and Bob in another.

Once we got to the tip of Australia, our next stop would be Thursday Island, just off the northernmost point of Australia and our jumping off point to Indonesia.

Whitsunday Islands, Barrier Reef, Queensland, Australia

Sailing up the northern Barrier Reef, Australia.

Into Primitive Land, The Spice Islands

The port authority on Thursday Island was very friendly, so we asked him for local knowledge on Indonesia. He said, "We don't have any. You're going into a primitive land." That was exactly what we wanted to do. While we were in Australia, I had the idea to follow the travel log of an old schooner that came out of Gloucester, the *Yankee.* I wanted to follow their route though eastern Indonesia and compare and contrast their notes from the mid-1930s to our own observations.

We decided to go up the western side of New Guinea and stop at the first islands of Indonesia we came to, the southeast Moluccas. We had generally decent sailing for our seven days crossing the Arafura Sea, through light winds, thunderstorms, and squalls. We arrived in the middle of the night into the little village of Tual. It was so strange. Their sailing vessels weren't powered or painted. The people wore sarongs. We didn't speak a word of their language and they didn't speak a word of ours. We anchored off the village and raised the American and Costa Rican flags, as we usually did.

We took turns keeping watch to prevent people coming aboard our boat. All of the locals would come out to our boat in their homemade boats and sit and stare at us. Possibly, they hadn't had any sailing visitors before. Carol had the morning watch when a man came alongside the boat and pointed toward the wharf. A couple of men holding guns wanted me to come ashore. I rowed ashore with our passports and papers, but our visas expired three months earlier. We had fallen behind on the itinerary we had planned back in Sydney.

A teak ketch in Indonesia carrying sweet potatoes.
The crew had never seen a nautical chart before.

Village of Tual—they had likely never seen an overseas boat before.

Outrigger with sails of woven mats.

Family and their sailing home.

Trouble

In short, the Indonesian government wasn't recognizing Tual as an official port of entry any more. They wanted us to go elsewhere. Carol had to go back to work in the States, so she took an inter-island flight on a six-passenger plane that landed and took off on a small grass field. It was going to be going to Ambon, the new official port of entry for the Moluccas Islands. When she arrived, officials said she didn't have a valid stamp on her passport for entering the country and detained her in their jail. Fortunately, on the plane she had met an island official who vouched for her and verified that she entered in Tual, so she was released. He also invited her to come and stay at his mother's house for a few nights till she

Contaminated water from our tanks.

could get another flight out to Bali en route to the States. After Carol had explained how she came into the country they sent out an Indonesian Navy boat to find Jane and me, but they never found us. We sailed to Ambon and dealt with the officials about entering the country.

Ambon was filthy. Jane and I couldn't risk going to shore together; we were sure the boat would be ransacked. Hundreds of local people living on their homebuilt sailboats were constantly watching us. But we needed water, fuel, and provisions. The water we got on Thursday Island was from a garden hose at a fuel dock and it was terrible. I asked the German man at the dock if anyone had run fuel through that hose and he said, "No, that's good water." I took a small sip and put it in the tank, only to realize later that it smelled of diesel.

We met a local student named Ali and he helped us find fuel and dry goods and took us around to the different offices we needed to find to clear out as fast as possible. Getting the proper visas for the various countries and clearing customs at entry ports was always a hassle. We always seemed to be in trouble but somehow got through it.

Chapter Seven

Indonesia to Seychelles

Forbidden Coast

JANE AND I SAILED DOWN to Wetar, an island just north of Flores. Our old sailing directions said there were fresh water streams on the island's north side. This was the "forbidden coast," with few villages and no real harbor. As we went further west, it looked more hospitable. We went close to shore, using the sailing directions to find the river. We found it. The beautiful, clear stream took a ninety-degree turn just before it emptied into the ocean. The island had no villages, no policemen, no official stamps, and no more people.

Jane and I stayed there for a couple days, thoroughly cleaning our water tanks and replacing them with clean river water. We added two tablespoons of bleach to every fifty gallons of water, killing all the bugs and giving it a sweet taste. Now we had good water, could do our laundry, wash ourselves, and relax in the river. It was a great relief just to be in a stream of fresh water.

Wetar Island— a clear, fresh-water stream for washing and filling our water tanks.

A Twelve-Hour Fight

We were about 800 miles from Bali, where we would exit Indonesia and go into the Indian Ocean. It was just Jane and I. We were constantly trolling for fish and ended up hooking a big one. I had a wire leader and tried pulling the fish in. He pulled the line right out of my hands. I thought it was a shark. We hooked it at ten o'clock at night and spent the rest of our night shifting watches trying to pull it in. He slowed our progress to about two knots; we were hardly moving. He swam, as he wanted to, dragging us backwards like a dog on a leash. At ten the next morning we finally got the fish close to the boat. It was an Allison tuna, a yellowfin that was as big as they get.

I asked Jane to get the gaff in his mouth or gill, and then we could use the halyard from the mainsail to try to haul him up or get a strap on him and hoist him aboard. Half his body was out of the water when the wire snapped. We were relieved to see him swim away. That night, we anchored off a village, and I spent the evening thinking, "We could have fed the whole village if we had just gotten that tuna."

In our migration through the northern chain of Indonesian islands, we came to a long island called Flores. We saw a steel vessel anchored there and learned that it was a Catholic mission ship supplying a village on the island. We asked if we could get some fuel from them. They said, "Of course, why not?" We topped off our tanks and bought some food that the ship had brought to the island's markets. Now we had enough fuel to motor the 400 miles to Bali, if necessary.

Lessons Learned in Bali

Jane and I spent the next week sailing, alternating watches—four hours on, four hours off—around the clock. We eventually came to Bali's Benoa Harbor. After a long time of not eating the food or drinking the water in Indonesia, we were told that Bali's was safe. We went to an outdoor restaurant and immediately got really sick with severe stomach cramps. We went to the local hospital a day or so later and the doctor said, "Well, it's the change of climate." I said, "We've been in the tropics now for two-and-a-half years, so I don't think it's the change of climate." He gave us codeine tablets, telling us to take ten a day, and we got better.

We never ate ashore in Indonesia again. We cooked our own food, boiled our own water. We ate a lot of rice and fresh fish whenever we could catch it, usually by spearfishing or trolling a line. We didn't have a refrigerator, but we had an icebox.

We needed to paint the bottom of the boat, so we found a guy who charged one dollar for his help and three dollars to rent the bamboo post to pry the boat up. The location we chose had a five-foot tide, so we brought the boat in until it was just touching the hard, sandy bottom at high tide. We rigged up six-inch diameter pieces of bamboo to hold it. When the tide went down, he and I worked from opposite sides, scrubbing from the water line down until the bottom was clean. As soon as

Haul-out Balinese style.

the tide reached the bottom, we painted back up again. Our plan worked well. We gave him a letter of recommendation, which he was very pleased with, and a one-dollar tip. We got the boat hauled out and painted for a grand total of five dollars.

Bali was inexpensive, densely populated, and a little more relaxed than other places in Indonesia. There were other nearby boats, so we'd all watch out for each other and take turns going ashore. Jane and I rented motorbikes and went to Denpasar city and Kuta Beach. When it was time to leave, we went without a government clearance. I just didn't want to waste another two days being frustrated in the port captain's office. Officials from one branch of government didn't recognize the authority of other branches. We'd go into one office and they would just mock whatever paperwork we had received at another. They ridiculed other officials and claimed we came in illegally. In Bali, we decided not to bother with it, stocked up on ice, meat, and Balinese rice, and headed southwest for Christmas Island, five and a half days away.

Christmas Island

We arrived at Christmas Island, which had no harbor, and anchored close to shore. We met the Australian port official and told him we didn't have a clearance from Indonesia. "You and everybody else," he said. "Don't worry about it. Half the boats that come in here leave Indonesia without a clearance." We anchored on the lee of the island off the rocky cobblestone shore. It was a tough anchorage, but it had a small yacht club nearby with beer in the fridge that they offered on the honor system.

At Christmas Island, heavy machinery and conveyors dug up and moved the pure phosphate coral rock that made up the island. The dirt made wonderful fertilizer and the phosphate business was in its heyday. Malays and Indonesians came there to work, bringing their entire families. In turn, they received housing and education.

We were treated very well for the five days we were there. The Aussies seemed to party all the time. Beyond work, that's all they had to do. We were invited out every night. The Aussies all drove cars and they lent us one, saying, "Fred got in a prang" (crash) "driving his car home a few months ago and broke both his legs. His car is fixed up; use that. He's in a hospital in Australia. He won't mind. He won't be driving for a while."

The island had a modern grocery store. There I was, in a pair of flip flops and cut-off pants, marching up and down the aisles while eating a frozen pie, crumbs falling on my feet. The grocery store's proprietor said, "You must be the new yachties that just came in." "You guessed it," I said. He offered to help any way he could and pointed us to the reasonably priced Australian food. It was a great place to provision, and we took full advantage. By the time we left, we had restocked our food, gotten some diesel oil, and topped up the water tanks. We felt pretty good.

Fairy Terns

We sailed 610 miles west-southwest further into the Indian Ocean, over to Cocos Keeling. There were no continents to protect us from the huge ocean storms that race right around the globe, stretching through the open ocean from south of Tasmania all the way around to Cape Horn. We faced gales from the southeast, driving twelve- to fifteen-foot swells from the south. We were being thrown all over the place. It was hard getting sights with the sextant. Jane and I traded off doing four-hour watches. Fortunately, the steering vane was working pretty well but I don't remember sleeping at all.

Unlike Christmas Island, which was fairly tall and visible from far away, Cocos Keeling was only as tall as a coconut tree. It's basically a huge atoll, about six miles across, pushed up a couple meters above the surface of the ocean. The Yanks built a landing strip on its far side during World

War II, and the Australians used it as a stopover place for long-range fly-ing. They had an aerodrome light, which was meant for planes, not boats.

We were dead reckoning towards Cocos Keeling and I was anxious to get a couple sun lines to get our position. We were sailing pretty fast, which was about six knots, and I was worried we might run right up on the island. The occulting light was only ninety feet up in the air on the other side of the atoll, the near side of which was much closer to us than the aerodrome light. I saw a reflection off a cloud that had a little flash to it, just a little spot of light in it now and then. I never wrote down the bearing, but I remember thinking, "That's the aerodrome light on Cocos Keeling. It's pretty much right in front of us." The seas were so rough, that after midnight, we hove to just so I could get some rest for about an hour.

I was waiting to see the island in daylight, which came around six o'clock but there was still no island. We got all the sails up, sailing pretty fast with lots of wind. I kept climbing the rigging to check for coconut trees. I eventually got some sun lines that put us pretty close to the island. Our portable radio was giving us a radio direction-finder signal from the aerodrome. The Morse Code signal for Cocos Keeling, "beep-beep, beep," kept getting clearer as we progressed. I kept going up and down the mast and eventually got a sight in the afternoon. I said to Jane, "I'm pretty sure we missed this place." If we were more than four miles off, we wouldn't have seen it.

After seeing the aerodrome light at 12:30 a.m. the night before, more than twelve hours had passed without reaching the island. We'd seen some booby birds the previous day, but they have a flight range of about 500 miles from any piece of land, so they aren't very helpful. Then we saw fairy terns, which told us we were within twenty miles of their nesting place. So, that was a good sign.

For about the tenth time, I went up the ratlines on the mast, hanging on to the gaff jaws on the mainsail. We went up on a big swell and I saw a flat line of trees right in front of us. It hit me like an electric shock. I started back down the mast, thinking I had imagined it. About halfway to the deck, I decided to look again. I held on for another minute or so, when, clearer and clearer, I saw the island group about four miles away. The steering vane brought us right into the entrance; we went in and anchored. It had taken us five days to get there.

Descendants of a Brit named John Clunies-Ross controlled Cocos Keeling. Ever since the first Clunies-Rosses landed there in 1827, his family and the islanders had been harvesting the island's coconuts. About 100 people lived on Home Island, one of the islands of Cocos Keeling, but the Clunies-Ross family didn't like foreigners visiting and influencing the islanders' perspective of the outside world.

There was a lot of controversy about gifts on the island. The Clunies-Ross family worried that foreigners bringing gifts would give the islanders the impression that life was better elsewhere. The family controlled the people, saying, "We'll provide you with a home. We'll provide you with a boat for fishing. We'll provide you some land to harvest coconuts. We'll provide your medical and educational needs for your whole life. And you can leave the island if you want, but once you go, you can never come back."

We had met some former Cocos Keeling islanders on Christmas Island. They had left the island, but could never return. They were always homesick. When they heard we were headed for Cocos Keeling, they loaded the forward end of our boat with tins full of gifts.

We anchored off of Direction Island. Eventually, an Australian boat came to us from the airstrip on the far side of the atoll. There was very little intermingling among the islands. The Australians maintaining the airstrip and the scattered yachties, like ourselves, weren't allowed to mingle with the Malays living under the Clunies-Ross family on Home Island.

The Aussies invited us to the far side of the island, where the anchorage wasn't as good. We stayed overnight at the magistrate's house. They offered us what they had. Jane and I were the lone yachties visiting. Now,

Cocos Keeling is a favorite stop for sailors on the traditional route. We stayed on Cocos, put the boat back in shape, and left on June 23, 1974.

Seas Over Mast

The Australian weather service warned us of a bit of a weather hellhole about 700 miles away from Cocos Keeling. It was about six days away, en route to Rodriques, but when we started out we sailed right into a gale of wind. We were in seas taller than our mast, with lots of water coming aboard. We had some tremendous crashes. Thinking back to that sail, I often wonder how the dinghy lasted on deck without being swept overboard. The wind and waves were so rough and loud that Jane and I just yelled back and forth to say that we were okay while on watch.

Seven days into the passage, the self-steering vane broke and we had to hand steer. I had carefully checked the trim tab, which is underwater, but the heavy load of the boat moving so fast against it broke it off. Because of the potential bad weather, I had put a large truck tire on the boat just in case we needed it as a sea anchor to slow us down in a following sea. (In a following sea, the boat is moving in the same direction as the waves.) I hoped the tire would keep us from pitchpoling—going end over end. For a couple days, we were surfing down the waves, so we had to put our anchor line in a big loop and put the truck tire over the side to keep the boat from surfing down the waves. We were taking care of the boat as best we could, but it was the roughest seas we had experienced to date. We just had to ride it out.

We began to realize that we would need to steer into the southerly swell if we wanted to make it to Rodrigues 1,700 miles away. All circumnavigators face trouble with the Indian Ocean. It's rougher and has a greater distance between islands than other oceans. The Society Islands in the southeast Pacific, where Jane and I met, were placid in comparison to the Indian Ocean. We were somewhere between fifteen and eighteen degrees south of the equator, but still in the convergence zone.

Because of the weather, we realized we couldn't make Mauritius, so we changed course downwind for Seychelles. I was using hand-drawn charts, made from conversations with other yachties, to find the harbors in Port Louis on Mauritius, and I had vague charts for Rodrigues, but I had no charts at all for Seychelles.

We alternated steering either three or four hours off and on. One day, I tried to get a sight and a wave went down the cabin hatch. It washed out our portable radio, which gave me the time ticks to get our position. Also, the saltwater meant we couldn't dry out any of our bedding. Everything down below was soaked.

After just seven days with a working steering vane, we spent the next fourteen days hand steering. We arrived in Mahé, Seychelles, after a twenty-one-day sail from Cocos Keeling. We were pretty wiped out. I went to sleep thinking, "I don't think we'll ever sail from here again." Jane had had enough and said she wasn't sailing any more. I was tired of it, too, and felt defeated. "Maybe we should sell the boat," I wondered. Fortunately, with a lot of rest and being in such a beautiful place, we were able to get the boat back in shape again and put the experience of the Indian Ocean behind us.

The USS *Paul*

We were outside the harbor getting ready to go to customs when a boat came out to meet us. They told us they wouldn't clear us and we had to wait a couple days. They wouldn't let us in the harbor. We were bobbing up and down in the outer anchorage when a US Navy destroyer, the USS *Paul*, passed by, clearing in right away. An Australian couple we knew from the Pacific came by on a dinghy, saying, "This is a good stop." They gave us some beer and told us to "forget about the port captain. Go in, get yelled at, get stamped, and you'll never see the officials again."

We cleared in the next day. We found out that Seychelles was in a drought and that they had only drinking water, the spigot for which was turned on for just an hour each day. They didn't want us doing laundry. We thought, "Holy smokes. Here we are, three degrees from the equator and we can't do our laundry." But our friend told us, "That Yankee destroyer out there has got plenty of water on it, believe me." The next day, I borrowed his dinghy and went a mile out to the destroyer. I told them our situation and they told us to come alongside the next day.

Alongside the USS Paul *in Seychelles.*

We brought our boat alongside the *Paul* and heard on the intercom, "Standby to receive." A long wait, then "Sailboat!" About thirty crewmembers lined up with these huge fenders. They tied us fore and aft and lowered down a two-and-a-half inch inside-diameter hose from a fire hydrant. I said, "Just crack it." While they were filling our water tanks, Jane started doing our laundry in a bucket. They said, "Send us up all your laundry, and by the way, come back for dinner tonight. We'll come and pick you up in the launch."

We ate in the wardroom with the captain and the officers, all in their dress uniforms. We hadn't seen a collection of Americans in a while and it was exhilarating. A lot of them were the same age as Janie and I, and they were halfway around the world. They had wives and family back home and they seemed so relaxed and happy to be there. I kept thinking, "What a contrast between how they came halfway around the world as compared to us." I had given them my parents' phone number and later found out that they had called them to say that we were in Seychelles and doing okay.

USS Paul *in Seychelles—Taking on water during shortage.*

The *Dwyn Wen*

We started looking for work, knowing we wouldn't get much pay there. We weren't allowed to take any job that the local Seychellois could do. I ran into a fellow who went through Hurricane Bebe with us in Fiji, a Swede captaining a schooner on weeklong trips around Seychelles for Lindblad Travel Agency out of New York City. The schooner was the California Yacht Club's flagship for forty-five years. It was 125 feet long and it had a crew of eight. It carried ten to twelve passengers a week for ten to twelve thousand dollars each time. Hans was the captain, but he was leaving, so he said to me, "I'll arrange for you to meet Sonja Lindblad. Maybe I can leave sooner, if you take over my job." He told me to wear my best clothes when I went to meet her. My best clothes were a well-worn shirt, shorts, and flip-flops, but I got the job.

Dream job as captain of 125-foot schooner yacht Dwyn Wen, *with a crew of eight.*

I had to go to the port captain's office to take an examination to prove I could navigate, which was pretty funny. Seychelles is out in the middle of the Indian Ocean. We were on an island group with just one harbor and one channel. We sat on either side of the captain's desk. He asked

Dwyn Wen *at anchor.*

Rene Bennoten, mate on Dwyn Wen.

questions like, "If you were going down this channel"—pointing at his desk—"and you wanted to pass that boat, what would you do?" I said, "Well, if I had a horn, I'd blow the horn once, and if he answered with one blast, I'd pass him on the right-hand side. If he answered with two blasts, I'd answer with two blasts, and pass him on his left-hand side." He threw a book down on our imaginary diagram, "What if there's a reef up here and a reef over there?" I said, "Well, in that case, I wouldn't pass him." "That's the right answer," he said, and with that, I got my British coxswains certificate.

With that certificate, I could operate a lifeboat on any British merchant ship. It also enabled me to captain the 125-foot schooner *Dwyn Wen*. The boat originated in Dartmouth, England, in 1906 but had been in Seychelles for four years. The crew of eight included two cooks, the captain, and an English-speaking hostess who took care of the passengers. We catered to wealthy people from all over the world. Sailing the Seychelles islands was "the thing to do" at the time. They're absolutely beautiful islands with pristine water. Spearfishing wasn't allowed there, so every time we stuck our heads in the water, we saw everything from turtles to tuna. We were allowed to spearfish only for octopus, using a two-foot long spear.

Jane visiting on La Digue.

Anchored off the small island of Cousin.

Chapter Eight

Seychelles to Israel

The Almost End

BECAUSE OF LOCAL EMPLOYMENT REGULATIONS, Jane couldn't get a job. We were eventually able to get into the well-protected harbor and we stayed anchored there. A nearby boat club had showers and a restaurant. We were fairly early in the season for crossing the Indian Ocean, but we recognized a few other visiting cruisers that came in and anchored near us. We had a good social life there. I seldom got off the *Dwyn Wen*, usually for five hours around Wednesday at noon, while the cleaning crew came aboard. At six o'clock, we'd have orientation with the new passengers, get underway again, and go anchor on an island nearby. Then we'd sail the twenty miles to Praslin Island. It was a continuous loop.

At the beginning, the weather was pretty rough, but we were on a 200-ton boat that anchored every night. We only sailed through the night once a week. I earned six hundred dollars a month, which was excellent pay for Seychelles. The crew earned twenty dollars per week. We encouraged the passengers to tip the crew. I thought of it as my adventure in paradise and the crew were working to support their families.

When we arrived in Seychelles, we were ready to sell our boat and fly back to the States. Everything seemed so grim. We were tired and broke. The boat needed new sails and was generally really beat up. I had a buyer ready to give me my asking price of ten thousand dollars. Then I got the job on the *Dwyn Wen* and every day got a little bit better. We felt more comfortable and were making some money again.

Eventually, a friend from school, Ed Dyment, finished building a house in Manchester, Mass., put down his tools, and flew to Seychelles. He wanted to sail up the Red Sea with us. He flew down with a one-way ticket, which meant a master of a boat had to immediately sign him on as crew. They quarantined him at Seychelles airport. Jane had to go down and sign the documents for his release. I'd been running the *Dwyn Wen* since July. We left on December 6, 1974 for Djibouti, Somalia.

Ed Dyment towing us over the equator in the Indian Ocean.

Ed Dyment steering.

Losing Omi

Entering the Gulf of Aden, we sailed through a rough and confused sea. Omi, our cat, used to go in the old dugout canoe, which we would tie to the deck. It had a rough, splintery bottom so she could hold on with her claws. But we got a new dinghy in Australia with a fiberglass bottom and she couldn't hold on as well. Water came over the rail all the time and she used to go on deck to look for fish and squid that would come flying aboard at night. On December 13th, at four in the morning, she was up on deck looking for breakfast. The boat took a big roll, and Ed thought he saw her tail go up but didn't see her body. She went off the top of the dinghy and overboard. She had gone overboard before when we were anchored, but never while we were at sea. We looked and looked but couldn't find her. It was overcast, it was dark, and it was a big sea running. We finally had to stop looking for her and move on.

Sailing Into a War Zone

People ask me why we decided to sail into a war zone. Well, by 1975 the fighting between Egypt and Israel, which started in the Yom Kippur War in 1973, was over. Israel controlled the Sinai Peninsula and the Suez Canal, which connects the Red Sea to the Mediterranean. We had information from the British that small boats were active in the canal doing support work, but there was no other traffic allowed to pass through. Our only other choice was to sail around the Cape of Good Hope, at the southern tip of Africa, adding 6,500 miles to the trip. We thought we'd give the Suez a try.

We left Mahé, Seychelles, and arrived in Djibouti, Somalia, in late December. We did the 1,500-mile run in fifteen days, non-stop, and crossed into the northern hemisphere for the first time in three years.

While in Djibouti we invited any three sailors from the frigate USS *Elmer Montgomery* over to dinner. The USS *Paul* had treated us so well,

Running up the Red Sea.

Anchored by ourselves at Great Hanish Island, Red Sea.

so we thought we'd return the favor. Three crew showed up with a case of beer, and we treated them to a homemade spaghetti dinner on the deck. In turn, we were invited aboard the *Montgomery* for Christmas and other occasions. They had just returned from Aqaba, Jordan, and gave us valuable information on the situation in the northern Red Sea. Israel controlled the entire Sinai and was guarding it with armed patrol craft. We had some old charts of the region, and the crew gave us some current ones that were very helpful. Our interest was to sail up to Suez and get thru the canal as soon as we were able.

We left Djibouti in early January with a clearance for Suez, but stopped at Port Sudan, about halfway up the Red Sea, where we tried to get Egyptian visas. No luck. No luck, either, trying to get any response from the US embassy. We sailed from Port Sudan waving goodbye to the East German captain of a tramp merchant ship who gave us some tinned food. I particularly remember the five-pound tin of butter.

Headwinds are the norm in the northern part of the Red Sea, so we beat our way for seven days, crossing to the Saudi side several times. In daylight, after sailing close to the coast after going by El Qusier, in southern Egypt, we took an anchorage in a small hole in the reef in hopes of getting some rest. We made no attempt to land and we did not fly a Q (quarantine) flag indicating our desire to come ashore.

A group of Egyptian soldiers came out from shore in a small boat. The leader, with a rifle in hand, ordered me into the boat, shaking his head and saying, "Bad, bad." Once ashore I was put in the back of a jeep, and we rode for many miles to a telegraph station next to an ancient prison with plenty of boisterous prisoners all waving their arms and yelling. The telegraph did not work, so I was escorted, with a soldier under each arm, back to the jeep and taken for a four-hour ride to the port of Safaga, where, from late at night until the next day, I was interrogated. I was very cold and wore my old military-style green jacket, which said "USC&GSS

Bedouins on Sinai Peninsula, Israel (now Egypt).

Oceanographer" on it. Someone gave me an Egyptian army jacket to put over it. I'm thinking, "This isn't good. They think I'm an Israeli spy or something."

I told the same story numerous times and also had written evidence that we had made contact with the British naval attaché, who were monitoring the clean-up of the Suez Canal, as well as a copy to the Egyptian naval authorities in Cairo. The information I provided included passport numbers, a description of our boat, and our itinerary sent from the Seychelles.

I was taken back to the boat to get more papers. Ed and Jane were now under military guard. I was brought back to shore and this time I was taken in the back of a dump truck to Hurghada. There, I finally got to speak English to a high-ranking military official who dialed the US embassy on a hand crank telephone. I remember him being somewhat amused when the embassy official told me that they would notify my next of kin. We were in a war zone, the US official said, and they could not help us any further even if they wanted to.

After all that, the Egyptians believed my story, but in the end, we were told to leave Egypt and make no further attempt to go any further north as it was mined, and soldiers along the coast had orders to shoot at any unfamiliar vessels. "And believe me," he said, "the enemy will do the same."

Ed needed to get off the boat and meet up with his wife. He rode a bus to Cairo where he got on a plane a few days later and flew to Crete. Jane and I, on the other hand, sailed on. As we crossed the Red Sea we got a rare south wind shift and headed up to the Straits of Tiran, Israeli controlled, where we were met by an Israeli gunboat at night. After much yelling and vigorous pointing to the American flag in the mizzen rigging, someone said in English, "Come right! You are going on the rocks!" The straits are half a mile wide and my chart showed only one lighthouse, but we were sailing between two lighthouses, one light on each end of the reefs. They let us proceed up the Gulf of Aqaba to Eilat.

We were lucky to get this far unscathed. Back in Djibouti, we had met up with several other yachties, and not all of them were so lucky. There was a German and a Frenchman single-handing with no engine, an Australian family on a steel boat, a second Australian boat, a New Zealand boat, and another American boat. Out of all those boats, only one made it to the Suez Canal. Two were shipwrecked on the way up the Red Sea and lost their boats. One returned to Australia. The other Australian boat was put under arrest in Safaga. We were told the crew was imprisoned for six months and later deported.

Chapter Nine

Israel to Gloucester

A Bad Joke

WE ARRIVED IN EILAT, ISRAEL'S southernmost port, in January 1975. I got a job on an oil pollution-control boat, a steel launch shipped over from New Orleans, Louisiana. It was built in the 1950s to bring customs officials out to arriving ships. I worked for a Lebanese guy, a Jewish-American fellow, and two Israelis. I didn't speak Hebrew or Arabic. The Lebanese boss spoke Hebrew and Arabic, but no English. The Israelis spoke Hebrew, a little bit of this and a little bit of that. The Jewish American spoke English and a little bit of Hebrew. The communication wasn't the best. We had to report and clean up any oil spills near Eilat, on the Israeli side of the Gulf of Aqaba. The few oil spills we found were fairly small. We brought oil booms out from shore and towed spills to the Jordan half of the Gulf, hoping the wind would blow it their way.

The operators on the boat weren't skilled, and the Port of Eilat wasn't well protected, so we were always banging into things. I soon realized that the other guys in the crew were smuggling TV sets, tape recorders, and other electronic equipment. They thought it was pretty cool; I disagreed. I had no desire to spend time in an Israeli jail for a tape recorder that went missing off some ship. I wanted no part of their extracurricular activities, so they would leave me on a barge or take me back to my own boat whenever they were smuggling. That arrangement worked out fine.

Our ship was illuminated, so any of our bosses could look into the Gulf at nighttime and see that our vessel was patrolling. We often snuck over to somewhere protected after midnight, tied up, and slept. Sometimes Jane would make us all dinner when we tied alongside *Peregrin Took*. Just before light, we'd idle back out into the bay, turn our lights on, and pretend we'd been there all night.

The Israelis had done some underwater demolition to sink Egyptian patrol boats in the port of Safaga. Fearing a counterattack from the Jordanian side, the Israelis used listening devices—headphones attached to hydrophones—to check for enemy underwater demolition teams that could blow up Israeli ships in port. Whenever the patrol ships heard anything, they would send out a craft and throw in handheld depth charges—basically a kilo of explosives on a ten-second timer—and then speed away. Jane, sleeping down below on our boat two miles away, would wake up with a start whenever these things went off.

One day, as a joke, a patrol boat set off a depth charge right next to us. They quickly sped off to get out of the way of the charge, but we were a heavy steel boat and couldn't move fast enough. We managed to get only about ten feet away from where they threw it, and the blast went off about twenty feet below our boat. It lifted our whole stern out of the water. We all fell over. The boat's steel plates, which weren't securely fastened down to the deck, went every which way. Someone could have gotten really hurt had those steel plates landed on us. The Israelis thought it was pretty funny, but we didn't. We were lucky none of us were hurt or the vessel damaged.

Crossing Israel

While we were in Eilat, we made some friends and had a comfortable place to tie up. We met two other American boats. Two teachers from Southern California, their twelve-year-old daughter, and her friend were onboard *Teacher's Pet*. They had sailed from Djibouti to Jeddah, Saudi Arabia, and then up to Eilat with *Mariah,* which had sailed out of Fort Walton Beach, Florida, with a retired military pilot, his wife, and their son onboard.

Since the Suez Canal was closed, we all needed to truck our boats across Israel to get to the Mediterranean Sea, so Jane found a truck one day in Eilat that was carrying a big piece of machinery. She asked the drivers if they could help ship our boats across the country. They agreed to truck all three boats at once for eight hundred dollars each. A crane picked the boats out of the water in Eilat and put them on a flatbed truck, which drove up along the Jordanian border, past the Dead Sea and the Sea of Galilee, and then over to Haifa.

Trucking the boat across Israel from Eilat to Haifa.

Arrival in Haifa.

Haifa, on Israel's Mediterranean coast, was perfect for us. We could stay there, get the boat rigged up, and sail when we were ready. The night after we arrived, the owner of the trucking company invited us to his house to watch our boat being put in the water on a nationwide broadcast. The story they told was of us being sent away from Egypt and welcomed in Israel. The broadcast was in Hebrew, but we understood the general theme.

A few days later, we started the process of getting a clearance from Haifa. They gave us the clearance but wanted to keep our passports. I refused, saying, "I'm not giving my passport to you, only to have it go missing." I told them I would be back in the morning to continue the process. But they had given us the clearance paper, so the next morning we just left.

As we left Haifa, we turned on our transoceanic radio again and heard the percussions of bombs going off on the Lebanese border. The fighting between Lebanon and Israel was constant. The BBC broadcast warned of scattered gunfire, but we could hear, down below on the boat, the thumping of large explosions carrying through the water.

The Med

We sailed for four and a half days to the harbor of Heraklion on the island of Crete—a totally different world. We were coming from a very tense situation in Israel, where every bag was searched in every building and military personnel were walking around with automatic weapons. On Crete, everyone was relaxed. There was no military presence. The women were all dressed in black, from the scarves on their heads to their ankle-length dresses to their shoes. We sent a few telegrams and ordered spare parts. We were pretty much out of money. They had an American Express office, which was the only way, at the time, to communicate with friends and family in the US.

Our sail to Malta took five days. The island is smaller than Crete—old, independent, and seemingly a mixture of everyone in Europe. They welcomed us into the harbor and we tied up in a very well protected place alongside other people wintering on their boats.

My older brother, Kirk, flew out to join us as crew. He had been working as an engineer on oil tankers and offered to help us sail across the Atlantic. He brought three thousand dollars with him, which was more money than we had made on our entire trip—combined! He said, "A thousand for the boat, a thousand for you guys, and a thousand for me." He said I could pay him back whenever I could.

We traveled around the old city of Valletta and the ancient city of Mdina. We rented motorbikes for two dollars a day and saw ruins from the thirteenth century. The Knights of Malta built these incredible, fortified cities to hold off invasion. No automobiles were allowed in the fort of Valletta, but we saw where Napoleon had briefly stayed. We reluctantly left Malta a few days later.

Malta.

Fighting the Wind

We wanted to go straight to Spain, but we got caught in a norther and were blown over to North Africa. We still had Israeli food onboard when we landed in Tunisia. If the Arabs there found Israeli items we'd be in trouble, so we anchored off the coast. We found a fairly protected, uninhabited place until we got underway again, only to meet another norther. We decided to sail to Tunis—Tunisia's capital and largest port.

We arrived in the port of Tunis late at night, with some guy screaming Arabic at us from a microphone in a nearby tower. We left the boat tied where it was and went down below. At three in the morning, immigration and customs met us saying, "Don't pay any attention to the guy in the tower. He doesn't understand that you don't speak Arabic." He directed us to a small harbor, where it was pleasant and inexpensive, and we were able to get fuel and supplies. When we left, the weather pushed us right back into another Tunisian port town: Banzart.

The officials at Banzart seemed happy to see us. They seldom saw overseas sailing boats, so they gave us a good welcome. It was an ancient city and much more laid-back than Tunis. We stocked up on pita bread, baked goods, fuel, and water. We left a few days later, sailing through constantly shifting winds to Spain's Balearic Islands.

The Ports of Spain

We came into Porto de Palma on the island of Majorca. The Spanish officials didn't give us any trouble clearing in, but they wanted a hefty fee for us to tie up at the marina. We asked if we could anchor instead, and they directed us back to the bay, where we stayed for a few days, resting and replenishing supplies.

Kirk looking for dinner on coastal Spain.

We got underway again, heading for the Mediterranean side of the Spanish mainland. One night, we anchored behind the island of Formentera and then sailed on to Alicante. At Alicante, we put our anchor over, backed into the quay, and put lines ashore. The quay is part of the main street and waterfront of the small, ancient, beautiful port town of Alicante. We could walk a plank onto our boat and everyone spoke very clear Spanish. I could understand every word they said.

Our engine was losing power, so I went to a diesel repair shop, where I met a fellow named Roberto. He told me step-by-step how to check the engine. I followed his instructions, figured out that the injector nozzles were the issue and brought them back to him. He said, "You'll have to order two injector nozzles from Madrid, they'll cost you over one hundred dollars, and you'll probably have to wait a week to get underway again." I didn't like that option, so he offered, "I have two injector nozzles here that have a different spray angle. You could try those out." I said, "We'll try them," For six dollars and a handshake, I got two injector nozzles that got us all the way across the Atlantic to Gloucester months later without issue.

We started day sailing toward Gibraltar, stopping at Cartagena, Aguilas, and Almeria. The winds were bad and the merchant and fishing traffic kept getting heavier as we neared Gibraltar. We were always aiming to make it to some port before it got dark. Kirk would get a hotel for about six dollars a night. We would shower, go out to dinner, and Kirk would sleep in the rented room. The next morning, we'd sail on to the next place.

We were sailing near some fellow with his wife or girlfriend on a Swan 50, a modern, well-built, expensive yacht. Every day, we would leave early in the morning and spend the day tacking back and forth in the wind. They would start out around 9:30, make one slant and head straight for the next destination. One time, we came in through a heavy thundershower. We spent the day running around the boat, taking down the sails. After all that rigorous activity, we finally came in and tied up next to them. They had already had cocktails and gone ashore for dinner. That was our boat compared to the Swan. In any case, we made Gibraltar on May 27, 1975.

The Straits of Gibraltar

From a distance, we saw the large rock that defines the peninsula. We replenished and left Gibraltar on June 3, with our sites on our next port: Gloucester, Massachusetts, about 4,600 miles away. We entered the Straits of Gibraltar, where the wind is either fair or foul. In our case, it had been blowing in from the Atlantic for days and we inched forward only one or two knots at a time. We were staring at the entire Atlantic in front of us as our sails started tearing in the wind.

We turned back to Gibraltar, stitched up the sail, rested, and then got back underway first thing the next morning. We sailed all day and arrived in Tarifa, a small Spanish fishing port, that evening. We found a bunch

Rock of Gibraltar.

of lines running out to moorings, took one, tied up, and went to sleep. We woke up to a port full of tied-up fishing boats, but no one complained about our presence. I went ashore, looking for a machine shop to fix a leaky exhaust fitting in the hull. One of the fishermen introduced me to some guys who ran a shop. They replaced our exhaust fitting for a couple of dollars. They couldn't have been nicer to us.

We left Tarifa in the morning and spent the next day and night dodging ships coming and going through the Straits. Eventually, we did get offshore. Once we left the Straits, the wind died down and shifted in our favor.

37 Days Across the Atlantic

We headed down to 27° North, toward the latitude of Miami, Florida, to take advantage of the trade winds that would carry us across the Atlantic. After six days of sailing, we tore the mizzen sail. We were near the Portuguese islands of Madeira, so we changed course to make a stop there and get it repaired. We went into the port at Funchal, on the main island, for two days to make the repair and get our last provisions. We left Funchal sailing usually in light winds for the next thirty-seven days. The boat was going so slowly that we could jump over the side and swim along, scraping off any weed or grass that was slowing the boat down.

We got into the routine of doing watches. I remember Kirk's growing anxiety. Every day, I got a sun line in the morning and a latitude line at noon to advance our dead reckoning position. And every day, Kirk would anxiously await the results of the noon sight to see how much progress we made in the last twenty-four hours. He would ask how far we went and I'd say, "We made 100 miles since yesterday."

"Great," he'd say. "That's good!"

I would tell him, "We made sixty miles south and forty miles toward Gloucester."

"Damn!" he'd say.

Every day was a huge frustration for him. He was used to a ship, which could time its arrival accurately. On *Peregrin Took*, we knew we would get to Gloucester; we just didn't know what month! Meanwhile, he had his girlfriend, Linda, waiting for him to get home so they could get married. She was a hospital nurse and had timed her vacation to coincide with the arrival date he had given her.

Somewhere in the Atlantic, 1,000 miles from land.

Homeward

After twenty-one days of fairly good sailing we saw the lighthouse on Bermuda, which gave me confidence in our position. Crossing from Bermuda to the mainland of the United States you have to cross the Gulf

Stream. The mix of temperatures in the water creates its own weather system. It's a moving wall of water.

Two days after we passed by Bermuda, a US Navy vessel, the *Sealift Mediterranean*, circled around us. We didn't have a radio that could transmit, just receive, so we wrote on the back of our charts, "33 days from Gibraltar. All okay. Bound for Gloucester, Massachusetts." Through a megaphone on their bridge, they yelled, "Do you want us to contact anybody in the U.S.A.?" I gave them my parents' phone number, and unbeknownst to us, they called right away, reporting our position as 400 miles east of Cape Hatteras and that all was well onboard. We later found out that there was a search going on for two other vessels that were in trouble. One was a sailing vessel still missing somewhere out in the Atlantic.

We crossed the Gulf Stream in fairly benign, stable weather. I knew we were near the Continental Shelf when we started seeing some offshore lobster buoys. We sailed over Georges Bank, and as typical of Georges Bank, the fog rolled in. For a couple of days, we were limited to visibility of anywhere from zero to two miles. I had few opportunities to get sights through the fog to figure out our position, but we could tell by the change in water color and the foghorns of the nearby fishing vessels that we were approaching Cape Cod. We saw gannets, seagulls, and tide rips, which told us pretty much where we were.

I remember telling Kirk, "If we don't make Nauset Light or Chatham Light before dark, we'll have to tack offshore and make our landfall tomorrow." Before long, we saw Nauset Light. That evening we were listening to the radio broadcasts for the first time in thirty-six days and caught bits of the weather report. It was a beautiful day. We steered north of Cape Cod, to sail into Massachusetts Bay.

We started recognizing some of the fishing boats, and word passed that we would be arriving soon. Jimmy Dudley, a childhood friend, and his wife, Elise, were out cruising around early and came over to greet us. My sister Jeri and her son John were at the beach in Magnolia and noticed a sailboat inside of Kettle Island and realized it was us. She alerted the rest of the family and all got into my father's lobster boat to follow us to Gloucester. We sailed on to Gloucester where we could clear into the country.

Once we reached Gloucester harbor, we notified customs and they instructed us to tie up at the state fish pier. They inspected our papers and vessel and asked if we had anything to declare. We said we did not. We had only purchased one nineteen-dollar wooden statue in Bali. The inspector said he had never had an overseas boat come in that didn't have something to declare. This was a first for him. Once we cleared, Carol and other family and friends came to join us. My old friend Michael Faherty offered to let us use his dock.

Coming home was exhilarating. Jane and I had been on our own for a long time. I was coming home, but for Jane it was different. Her hometown was Seattle and she didn't know anyone in Gloucester except Carol and my parents. Gloucester was a place she had only heard about. But we were back in the States and we had made it. We were relieved.

Arrival Gloucester, Mass.—Customs tells us, "You can't get there from here."

On the day we got back, as we rounded Race Point on the tip of Cape Cod, I was thinking about how lucky we had been. We survived many storms in the South Indian Ocean, were always able to find work, and had somehow managed to get out of Egypt and into the Mediterranean. I always felt someone or something out there was watching over us. We were simply—sometimes not so simply—coaxing *Peregrin Took* towards her next destination, and if the gods were favorable, we would eventually arrive.

Carol and Jane at the state fish pier, upon arrival in Gloucester.

When we tied up at the state fish pier in Gloucester, our home-built Tahiti ketch had sailed over 32,000 miles. It had taken three and a half years. *Peregrin Took's* journey and our adventure were over—for now.

Photo published in The Boston Globe.

Made in the
USA
Monee, IL